8.99

DISCERNING THE SPIRIT OF THE AGE

Discerning the Spirit of the Age

Derek J. Tidball

KINGSWAY PUBLICATIONS
EASTBOURNE

Unless otherwise indicated, biblical quotations are
from the New International Version © 1973, 1978, 1984
by the International Bible Society. Inclusive
language version 1995, 1996.

ISBN 1 84291 062 0

Published by
KINGSWAY COMMUNICATIONS LTD
Lottbridge Drove, Eastbourne BN23 6NT, England.
Email: books@kingsway.co.uk

Book design and production for the publishers by
Bookprint Creative Services, P.O. Box 827, BN21 3YJ, England.
Printed in Great Britain.

Contents

Introduction

Coca-Cola, McDonald's, Disney and Nike are among the best-known names in our world. Their signs and logos are virtually omnipresent. They, together with a few other companies, increasingly provide what we drink, eat, wear, enjoy, want and find acceptable. They also shape the way we think. They not only provide us with commodities, they provide us with mindsets and worldviews. They mould the spirit of our age.

Paul wrote much to the Colossian and Ephesian Christians about the rulers, powers and authorities they feared in the heavenly realm. He instructed these young believers about the superiority of Jesus over them all. I have no doubt that in using those terms he had in mind supernatural beings who exercised an influence, often for ill, over people's lives. But I am also sure that he was refer-ring to human institutions, essentially the political authori-ty of Rome and the religious institution of the synagogue, which determined how people lived and thought. In our day, demonic and angelic beings still do their work, for good or ill. And so too do the more ordinary structures of the government, the economy, the commercial sector and the media. Among these 'powers and authorities' in our world global corporations, like those mentioned above, are primary. They send out compelling messages that fashion the way we see things, even if those messages are so subtly expressed that we are not always particularly conscious of them.

As Christians we are called to be 'in the world but not of it'. To be a disciple of Jesus is, by definition, to be counter-cultural. So we should be asking ourselves what implications these global businesses have for us and in what ways we need to exercise discernment so that we might resist the spirit of the age and live faithfully before God.

An older generation might have referred to this issue as one of 'worldliness'. It sounds a rather quaint word today – one that has gone out of fashion along with starched collars, corsets, the magic lantern, the wireless, wind-up gramophones and manual typewriters. Worldliness was easily defined before the social and moral revolutions of the 1960s. A few places and activities were labelled 'worldly'. As long as one avoided these – the pub, the cinema, the dance hall, the betting shop, or smoking, drinking, dancing and gambling – one avoided the sin of worldliness, or so it seemed. Each of these places, or activities, was significant in its day. Christians opposed them for a reason. But the approach was somewhat superficial. What this approach never did was address the attitudes these institutions gener-ated nor the more significant philosophies that were the engines of culture.

With the coming of the sixties the talk changed. Christians became concerned about relevance more than worldliness, involvement rather than separateness, engagement rather than distinctiveness. As a result, perhaps, disciples of Jesus became just like everyone else. And along with losing our distinctiveness, we lost our cutting edge. We forgot that our calling was not to converse with the world but to convert it. We were so busy bending over backwards to accommodate the world that we fell into it.

My plea is not a reactionary one. I do not want to resurrect the battles of the past. The 'spirit of the age' today wears different clothes than it did half a century ago. It's all too easy to maintain an avoidance of things previous generations of Christians have regarded as worldly while imbibing wholesale this generation's spirit of the age. Every generation needs to be able to recognise the garb in which contemporary worldliness is dressed. We need discerning minds to know how to avoid being sucked into the spirit of *our* age, and, equally, so that we do not unnecessarily or naïvely oppose things just for the sake of doing so.

In the chapters that follow we look at five powerful symbols that astute observers of our culture have pointed out as highly significant. Three are global corporations we have all encountered in some form: Nike with its slogan 'Just do it!'; Disney with its creation of a magic kingdom; McDonald's with its championing of fast food. Two are cultural metaphors of our time: the consumer and the tourist. Each of them has had a serious, and frequently detrimental, impact on the way we live as disciples of Jesus and relate as members of the church. We need to unmask them in order that we might live faithfully. The final chapter takes up a different metaphor and encourages us to be adventurous and creative in our understanding of how the church should function today.

I owe a debt of gratitude to a number of people: first, to Victoria Baptist Church, Eastbourne, whose invitation to conduct their houseparty on what it means to be the church in the twenty-first century began my thinking along these lines. Their reaction encouraged me to pursue the matter further. Then, to Scripture Union, who recently published a collection of essays by the faculty of LBC called *Christian Life and Today's World*, edited by Anna Robbins. They gave me permission to use my essay on consumerism in a slightly amended form here. I am grateful to my wife for so much, but especially, on this occasion, for composing the questions at the end of the book. I am also grateful to my friend Simon Johnston for reading and commenting helpfully on the drafts. As a future leader in God's church I pray that he may always prove faithful as well as relevant. Lastly, I am grateful to Richard Herkes and his colleagues at Kingsway for their encouragement and hard work on this little book. But none of these, of course, is to be held responsible for the views expressed or the mistakes that remain.

The book is written in the hope that we might move a little closer to fulfilling Paul's wish when he wrote: 'Brothers and sisters, stop thinking like children. In regard to evil be infants, but in your thinking be adults' (1 Corinthians 14:20).

1.

'Just Do It!' or 'Jesus Did It!'?

When you buy Nike footwear you buy more than something to wear on your feet: you buy a way of life. The company that came from nowhere now dominates the world, especially the global sports culture. Its famous, omnipresent logo, the swoosh, has become so familiar that for a period Nike did not even need to use its name when advertising. The logo said it all. Its slogan, 'Just do it!', has become part of everyday conversation and crops up routinely in the media. Its designer label is envied, as every parent knows. Any old trainers will not do. Any old sports shirt is not acceptable. It has to be Nike. The right label is all.

Christian disciples buy Nike products like anyone else. I myself have a pair of Nike shoes, which I wear when playing badminton, though they don't seem to help. But Christian disciples are not so aware that Nike's products and its advertising are not spiritually neutral. They are preaching a worldview and advocating a philosophy, albeit a complex one, that we can drink in without realising it.

Buy the shoes, purchase the shirt, by all means, but should we buy into the values of the company as well?

In the beginning, before Nike, was Blue Ribbon Sports. Founded in 1962 by Phil Knight, with help from Bill Bowerman, a sports coach and footwear designer, it first imported and distributed Tiger sports shoes from Japan. They employed their first staff member in 1965 and opened their first retail outlet a year later. Then Knight decided to market his own brand of shoes; shoes made to Bowerman's specifications. To do so the company needed a makeover. So Knight paid an art student called Carolyn Davidson the princely sum of $35 to design a logo that would portray an upbeat image of speed and movement, which he was confident his shoes would deliver to those who bought them. At the same time an employee, named Jeff Johnson, suggested the company change its name to Nike, after the winged Greek goddess of victory. Phil Knight was not particularly enamoured with either the logo or the name, but he went along with them.[1]

Steve Prefontaine, an American record-holder, was the first major athlete to wear Nike shoes in 1973, followed some five years later by the tennis player John McEnroe. In 1979 Nike-Air cushioning shoes were introduced and captured 50 per cent of the American market. A further boost came when 58 Nike-supported athletes won 65 medals at the 1984 Los Angeles Olympics, including Carl Lewis, who won four golds. With Michael Jordan of the Chicago Bulls endorsing its products from the mid-80s, the company was made.

---

1 Robert Goldman and Stephen Papson, *Nike Culture* (Sage Publications, 1998), p. 16. See also www.nikebiz.com

Within less than 20 years it was globally recognised and the business had leapfrogged its competitors to become the largest designer and marketer of athletic footwear, sports apparel, accessories and equipment in the world. In 1997 it grossed over $9 billion and had taken command of over 43 per cent of the athletic footwear business, pushing Reebok, its chief rival, into second place, with a market share of only 30 per cent, and consigning Adidas and Fila firmly to third and fourth positions. By 1996 it was offering 1,200 models of shoe entailing approximately 3,000 variations of colour and style. By then it was changing the designs almost every week.[2]

Nike's success is attributable to a number of factors. It has branched into new products, like ladies sportswear and athletic equipment. It has found new markets around the world. It has outplaced the production of its merchandise, limiting itself to designing and marketing only. This, of course, has had its downside, since it has led the company into major controversy over whether it is exploiting workers in third world countries, using sweated labour and profiting by not paying just and equitable wages.[3] It is good, indeed almost prophetic, at signing up new sports superstars like, in recent years, Tiger Woods. It has used wise business strategies, made deals and used sponsorship to good effect. Nike says the formula for success is quite simple: 'It all comes down to this: helping athletes perform.'[4] But the real secret of its success is the fact that it doesn't

---

2 Goldman and Papson, *Nike Culture*, pp. 5–6.

3 See Naomi Klein, *No Logo* (Flamingo, 2001), pp. 328, 350, 365–79 and 405–6.

4 www.nikebiz.com

sell products, it sells a brand. Its advertising has seduced a global market into thinking it must purchase the brand to belong, to be cool, to be taken seriously, to share in the victory. It has stamped an image on the minds (and sometimes the bodies) of millions, especially the young, conjuring up shades, one vaguely thinks, of 'the mark of the beast'.

The gospel according to Nike

Nike's advertisements not only keep the swoosh highly visible, and sell the shoes or shirts in mega quantities, they also sell the way of life the brand symbolises. The advertisements are the equivalent of the Nike scripture. It is there that the Nike message is to be found. Often focused on celebrities, it puts forth a vision of a 'celebrity democracy' in which all of us, whoever we are, can become the heroes. There is a mock reverence about the advertisements and they make use of a good deal of biblical language and a number of spiritual allusions as well. The adverts are the gospel according to Nike. So what is the gospel they proclaim?

'Just do it!'

One disciple of Nike, Carmine Collettion, a young Internet entrepreneur, had the Nike swoosh tattooed on his navel. He explains, 'I wake up every morning, jump in the shower, look down at the symbol, and that pumps me up for the day. It's to remind me every day what I have to do, which is "Just do it!".'[5]

---

5 Klein, *No logo*, p. 52.

'Just do it!' is the rallying cry that rouses people to get up off their couches and play sports. It summons them to shake off lethargy, put aside all potential restraints and inhibitions and get involved. It invites people to take control of their lives rather than be controlled by their misfortunes. It calls for them to break out of the dullness of their routine, mundane lives and achieve. It inspires them with a vision that just as super-athletes have conquered, they too might accomplish greater things and even perform with excellence. The call is motivational and inspirational. It says, 'No more rationalizations and justifications, it's time to act.'[6]

The cry has been particularly directed in recent years to those who have more than average reason for believing that they cannot 'just do it'. The obstacles of gender, race, age and disability are all exposed as insufficient reasons for doing nothing. Take gender as an example. Nike has invested much in advertising for the women's market, starting with Stacy Allison, the first woman to climb Mount Everest, and Priscilla Welch – 'former smoker, drinker and couch potato turned into champion long-distance runner' – in the late 1980s.[7] The advertisements have sought to communicate to women in language they appreciate rather than simply following the way of men. Hero worship has therefore become less significant, while appeals to the inner being and advertisements of a more reflective, therapeutic kind have become more prominent. They have also sought to follow the trends in women's sports and cater for the diversity involved, from the keep-fit leisure market to

6 Goldman and Papson, *Nike Culture*, p. 20.
7 *ibid.*, p. 119.

the more aggressive and competitive team games of women's volleyball, basketball and soccer.[8]

Throughout the 1980s and 90s advertisements portrayed senior citizens actively pursuing vigorous sporting achievements. Here were men and women who had refused to give in to age, curl up on their sofas or devote themselves to playing bingo. 'In the Nike philosophy the only limit to physical achievement is one's lack of will.'[9] Nor is coming from the wrong side of the track any excuse. The 'Time of Hope' advertisement depicted people of all backgrounds – poor and black as well as white and middle class, ghettoised and suburbanised, amateur and professional, free and wheelchair bound – striving to achieve, and succeeding.[10] The message is clear: no one need succumb to injustice, adverse circumstances or prejudice. We can all, if we choose, 'just do it!'.

Sport is the new religion[11]

Sport is portrayed as taking over where traditional religions that have failed left off. The game is presented as sacred. The sports stadiums are the new temples of worship, and sacred rituals take place within. The body has become the object of worship, and the swoosh has taken the place of the cross. Sport has become a means of secular salvation.

Sport offers the experience of transcendence. It allows people to reach out beyond themselves and enjoy another

---

8 The full picture is found in *ibid.*, pp. 118–45.

9 *ibid.*, p. 151.

10 *ibid.*, p. 69.

11 For the following section see especially *ibid.*, pp. 62–6, 146–53.

level of consciousness beyond the mundane, routine and earth-bound. It provokes awe and inspires adoration. It connects individuals with a force greater than themselves.

Sport offers individual redemption. It is a way of attaining inner peace and being fulfilled. In sport people come to find their true identity and know themselves. They can escape the disabling pressures of the rat race and of the urban, industrialised world and find healing from the crippling effects modern society has on what it means to be truly human. It enables people to be themselves. It ministers emotional wholeness and well-being. It provides instant karma.

Sport offers the healing of divisions. It balances the individual with community. It celebrates individual achievement and team success. One finds oneself while belonging to a community of others who also play the game. The most explicit example is found in the ideals of the Olympic Games, where dedication to athletics transcends all racial and political barriers and unites 'the family of man' in a global unity. Sport brings people together in a way nothing else does. Politics, business, education, technology and even religion divide. Sport reconciles.

Sport re-enchants the world. It's a well-worn theme that the world is not the enchanted place it used to be. Science and technology explain the world in mechanistic terms and leave little room for mystery. Religious interpretations of the world are dismissed as superstitious. We have created a rational, ordinary world where once a divine, supernaturally seasoned one was thought to exist. But sport still provides those moments of magic and connects people with the vital animating force of nature in a way that evokes mystery.

Sport requires the exercise of spiritual discipline. To achieve, the individual has to subject the body to discipline and punishment. There is no gain without pain. It's sacrifice that leads to fulfilment, as much as it ever did.

Yet, in contrast to traditional religion, it provides an '*à la carte* spirituality'.[12] Neither sport nor the Nike publicity machine claims to preach a single road to heaven. Unlike traditional religion it does not say, 'This is the way.' It is neither specifically authoritarian nor guilt-inducing. Choice is the order of the day. It provides the seeker with a number of options, and facilitates their discovery of which is right for them through experimentation. Individuals remain the judge of what's right for them. It's morality *lite*.

Effort conquers all

The four-letter word 'work' is a frequent one, at least by implication, in the vocabulary of Nike. Religious experience does not just happen. Achievements don't rain down from the sky, like a visitation from heaven. Effort, grit, determination, toughness, dedication, work, discipline and perseverance are all required if success is to be experienced. People need to be hungry to win. The price tag of victory will be suffering and pain. Sacrifice is the name of the game.

A typical expression of this work ethic is found in the advertisement starring Penny Hardaway, Orlando Magic's superstar basketball player, who intones:

Nah! I wasn't born with a basketball in my cradle.
For some believe we come out dunking once we are conceived.

---

12 Goldman and Papson, *Nike Culture*, p. 147.

Superstar? I got it made, right?
I went from nothing to something overnight.
Well, don't believe the hype.
I had to work to get to where I'm at and that's a fact.
Mom and Grandma raised me to be proud
and instilled their philosophy in me
knowing that no one could take that from me.
Nah! *I had to work* to get here.
At the Boys and Girls club. At Memphis State
I had to work to be great.
Just do it.[13]

The origins of this work ethic go back to the Reformation and especially to the teaching of Luther and Calvin (who themselves could legitimately trace it back to the Bible). They saw all of life, whatever one's occupation, as a vocation before God. It wasn't only the priests who were 'called'. It was the carpenters, bankers and scientists as well. Therefore life was to be lived responsibly before him and to be accounted for before him. Talents and time, gifts and resources all had to be used to the full, without waste and let-up, for his glory. Disconnected from these spiritual roots, however, the work ethic becomes a despairing and hard taskmaster. All the effort is directed at glorifying oneself. All the reward is in the here and now. Nothing is of eternal or divine significance.

Winner takes all

It is a logical extension to Nike's version of the work ethic to believe that winning matters. The pious rhetoric of the American sports commentator, Grantland Rice, has been

---

13 Cited in *ibid.*, p. 98, italics mine.

dumped in the dustbin of history. He wrote:

> For when the One Great Scorer comes
> To write against your name,
> He marks – not that you won or lost –
> But how you played the game.

In its place Nike tells us, 'If you're not there to win, you're a tourist.' 'If you can't stare down your opponent, if you blink, you don't have the will necessary to win.' You must win at all costs. Dominating your opponent is what it's all about. Whatever pleasantries are uttered elsewhere about us all being brothers and sisters together through sports, especially in the Olympic movement, the reality is different. Winning is what counts. Not only does one have to win without showing any mercy to one's opponent, but one has to look and behave like a winner, a celebrity of sorts, too.

Why Jesus would like Nike

There are some aspects of Nike's philosophy that disciples of Jesus can applaud. Christians can be an inhibited bunch, fearful of putting a foot wrong before God and, in a misguided attempt to please him, find themselves over-restrained by rules, just like some of the Pharisees of Jesus' day. They become shy of taking any risks whatsoever. But to live like this often indicates a lack of faith in the providential care of the sovereign Lord. It flies in the face of the godly wisdom of Ecclesiastes, which instructs its readers: 'Go, eat your food with gladness, and drink your wine with a joyful heart, for it is now that God favours what you do'

(Ecclesiastes 9:7). It also ignores the warning of Ecclesiastes when it points out the folly of being over-cautious: 'Whoever watches the wind will not plant; whoever looks at the clouds will not reap' (11:4). If we are over-cautious, always holding back because of some misfortune that might strike us, we shall never do anything. There are times when we should 'just do it'.

This slogan is particularly pertinent in a culture that seems to wallow in victimhood. Many lives are blighted by a false fatalism. People believe that because of injurious experiences in their childhood, or traumatic experiences in their youth, they are condemned to limp through life as emotional cripples. Many of us are looking for someone else to blame to excuse us from taking responsibility for our lives and to explain why we shouldn't really be expected to do anything to change our situation. Even some professionals whose jobs involve facing hazards, like those in emergency services, want to portray themselves as victims today (perhaps in order to gain compensation) when previous generations would have simply taken the dangerous aspects of their job in their stride. Nike has been right to debunk the folly of this argument and show that we do not have to be held captive by our past, our circumstances or our disabilities. Its strategy has been to shout this message both through its slogan, 'Just do it!', and by publicising the success stories of those who have overcome adversity in their lives. And its message, preached from a hundred different advertisements, has been timely.

This 'just do it' attitude might also be said to find parallels in the ministry of Jesus. The religious professionals of his day thrived on reinforcing the handicaps of those who didn't measure up to their own standards of spiritual fitness. The unclean, the poor, the disabled, the tax collectors and the sinners did not matter to God, or so they said, and had no right to his attention. They didn't want them to get up off their spiritual couches and approach him. Jesus, in contrast, invited 'the poor, the crippled, the lame, the blind' (Luke 14:13) – the very ones the Pharisees and other religious virtuosi excluded as unfit – to sit down at the banqueting table of the Messiah. They had no need to hold back. They were the very ones who were welcome. For the man Jesus healed at the pool of Bethesda it was a literal call to 'Get up! Pick up your mat and walk' (John 5:8). He had so blamed others for his inability ('I have no-one to help me . . . While I am trying to get in, someone else goes down ahead of me' [John 5:7]) that it took a sharp command from Jesus to break through the layers of rationalisations that kept him tied to his mat instead of experiencing the healing power of God. What he did literally was symbolic of what multitudes of others need to do spiritually, then and now. They need to get up off the couch and take a step of faith and accept his invitation, because God's grace is for them.

Jesus and Nike in conflict

While it is true that traces of the attitude of Nike might be reflected in the ministry of Jesus, the greater truth is that, at a more fundamental level, the way of life advocated by Nike clashes with the way of life advocated by Jesus. The fact that there might be some superficial connections, like those above, has led too many Christians to imbibe Nike's whole philosophy of life in an unthinking manner. But the Nike world has much more in common generally with the religion espoused by the Pharisees than with the teaching of Jesus. Let's look more deeply at it, this time through the filter of part of the Sermon on the Mount (especially Matthew 5:3–10).

Blessed are the rich in spirit versus *blessed are the poor in spirit*

Nike's philosophy is based on the idea that we already have within us all the resources we need to be achievers. The problem does not lie in the fact that we are unable to get off the couch and go for gold. It lies in the fact that we don't want to. Our problem is not inherent, not constitutional, but motivational. We have all the inner resources we need if only they can be matched by inner resolve. We are self-sufficient. We are rich in spirit. We must simply learn to tap into our inner wealth. We don't need to reach out to anyone beyond to help. We only need to reach within to win. We have the capacity to supply the determination, grit, effort and skills we need ourselves. It's all there. Our own works can save us.

According to Jesus, such a line of argument is deeply flawed. It is not those who are rich in their own spirits who are blessed, but those who are poor in spirit – those who know how spiritually bankrupt they are and recognise their inability to make up the shortfall themselves – who are blessed. The latter, not the former, are those who enter the kingdom of God. The problem is more than motivational. It is constitutional. There is a deficiency within our lives that we cannot supply ourselves. Only the grace of God from outside can supply it. We can't be saved by our own effort.

Jesus' parable of the Pharisee and the tax collector says

it most clearly (Luke 18:9–14). The Pharisee was conscious of what he could offer God from his own well-endowed spiritual investments. He boasted of his moral superiority, his religious observances and his generous alms-giving. In reality, however, as Jesus said, this man was not praying to God. He was 'praying about himself'. His prayer was one long glorious self-advertisement. The tax collector, whose loyalty to his fellow Jews would have been severely questioned and who, because of his profession, would have been an outsider while living among his own, knew he had no spiritual credit of his own to offer God. His personal and spiritual bank account was empty, whatever the truth of his financial bank account. Consequently he reached out beyond himself to God and simply begged for mercy, asking God to exercise pity on his life. He was the one, not the Pharisee, whose prayer God answered.

Never has any generation in history had so much, materially and in other ways, as Generation X. Yet never has any generation lacked as much in self-esteem as Generation X. A whole industry of therapists, pop psychologists and counsellors has been born as a result of the feelings of inadequacy those in their 20s and 30s experience. Techniques galore have been invented to improve people's self-worth; positive strokes galore are administered to improve people's self-image; and positive affirmations galore are dispensed to make people feel good about themselves. But it doesn't seem to improve the situation. Perhaps it is because the effort is ultimately misdirected. Perhaps we, like Nike, are telling people that they've got all they need within themselves; that they are self-sufficient; and all they need is to believe in themselves and 'just do it'. And the fact is they haven't got what it takes inside of them. The truth is that unless they are in touch with the living God, in whose image they were made and to whom they were designed to relate, and until they face their bankruptcy before him and discover his grace which covers all their shortcomings, they will never genuinely 'feel good'.

At the heart of the gospel is the fact that we can get back in touch with our Creator because of what Jesus has done for us. It is not a self-help gospel. It is about Jesus supplying what we lack. He made the connection we could not make ourselves. He alone has offered the perfect inward obedience that we, as fallen human beings, are incapable of offering to God. He alone maintained an unblemished relationship with his Father. His perfect self-offering led him eventually to a cross where, in apparent defeat, he made possible the restoration of the broken connection between God and his creatures. When he emptied himself completely and submitted to being crucified in weakness, he made salvation available. It is 'through his poverty' that we 'become rich' (2 Corinthians 8:9). Our poverty of spirit is matched by his richness of grace. But we can never receive that while we're full of our own abilities, our own potential, our own goodness and our own strength.

What matters is not that we can 'just do it', as if we could, but that 'Jesus did it'.

Blessed are the celebrities versus *blessed are those who mourn*

Nike builds a world characterised as a 'celebrity democracy'. The celebrities are the achievers, the ones who have made it. They are the ones we'd like to imitate because they have success, status, personality and, above all, money. Their spin doctors make sure their faces are seen in the newspapers and on the TV; for a fee, of course. Their publicity machines portray them having what we want. They are good for a laugh. For them, life is fun. They're the sort you'd want to come to a party to spice it up a bit and help you have a good time. They're the people who go from one exciting event to another, from one high to another. They pretend they're problem free.

The truth may be very different. The personal lives of many celebrities are a failure and their failures sometimes break through to public consciousness, as yet another marriage ends in acrimony, or another spell at a drug rehabilitation centre commences. Such uncomfortable truth is usually hidden from our view since it tarnishes the image of the celebrity world. But it is there nonetheless.

Nike tells us we can all be like these celebrities, if we try. Celebrity status is open to all to apply for, if we 'just do it'.

In contrast Jesus tells us that the ones who are truly happy are not the celebrities but those who grieve. To mourn, as Don Carson puts it, is to 'be understood as the emotional counterpart of poverty of spirit'.[14] It is to be distressed at what we do not have, rather than to boast about what we have. It is to lament that we are not what we should be, rather than to celebrate what we are. It's the opposite of being a celebrity before God. More widely, to mourn is to express pain at the state of our society and our world, riddled as it is by hurt, injustice, evil and immorality. It is to turn to God in tears, pleading for him to sort out the mess of our lives, without any proud illusion that we can sort it out without him.

---

14 Don Carson, *The Sermon on the Mount* (Baker, 1978), p. 18.

The kingdom of God is not made up of celebrities. They are usually too big to enter. It's made up of the small and the weak, who hurt for the brokenness of God's creation and cry out for redemption. Celebrities usually have too much of their own to be concerned about to bother with that.

Blessed are the pure in body versus blessed are the pure in heart

In the kingdom of Nike the body becomes the object of self-worship. It is through excelling athletically that you have a religious experience. Your own physical achievements are the means of transcendence, of escaping the strictures of this world and being in touch with something greater than yourself. The physical is the vehicle not only of fulfilment but of salvation.

This attitude is widespread and found well beyond Nike. The body is exalted throughout our society from a thousand different angles. Models have become the new goddesses and their thinness the object of widespread envy. Fitness centres have sprung up everywhere, so that each week we can be briefly helped to combat the ravages of our otherwise unhealthy lifestyles. In many churches more time is given to keep-fit classes than to prayer. 'Dieting for Christ' and 'Trim for Him' is what discipleship is about. As Os Guinness commented a few years back, 'With spiritual narcissism so well advanced, "Firm believer" is a matter of aerobics rather than apologetics, of human fitness rather than divine faithfulness. Shapeliness is now next to godliness',[15] whereas our grandparents once thought cleanliness

15 Os Guinness, *The Gravedigger File* (Hodder & Stoughton, 1983), p. 87.

was. Cosmetic firms ply their wares. L'Oreal tells us it's 'because you're worth it'. Cosmetic surgery is a growth industry because many want to stave off physical decay and pretend they've found the secret of eternal youth. Body art is fashionable. Sex is the be all and end all of existence, or so the media would have you believe, and sexual desire must be instantly gratified. The body is central to our understanding of ourselves these days.

To exalt the body in this way is self-indulgent idolatry. It is to worship what was created instead of worshipping the Creator. It is only another manifestation of the hubris that men and women have consistently displayed in history. It is an attempt to become gods and to construct a universe independent of the living God. It's as old as the Tower of Babel, where people thought they could construct their own way of reaching heaven and making a name for themselves, not then through their bodies but through their bricks and buildings (Genesis 11:1–9).

The body is not insignificant for Christians. Previous generations of Christians have often quite wrongly devalued it. Some of them fell into the error of equating the physical and the material with the sinful and the unspiritual. Such attitudes led to many Christians falsely believing sex was dirty and to adopting forms of physical asceticism that encouraged an escape from the body, as if they would bring us nearer to God.[16] Some wrongly oppose the spirit (which is considered good and spiritual) with the body (which is considered evil and unspiritual). The misunderstanding partly comes from the way in which older versions of the New Testament used the word 'flesh' to denote

---

16 On the latter see Paul teaching in, for example, Colossians 2:23.

our sinful nature. But, God created us as flesh and blood human beings and named us the summit of his creation (Genesis 1:26). He made us as sexual beings (Genesis 1:27–28). The incarnate Christ was embodied in human form (John 1:14; 1 John 4:2). His resurrection did not mean he became a spirit but that he assumed a new body. We are not going to be resurrected as souls but as transformed and incorruptible bodies (1 Corinthians 15:35–57). Paul teaches that our bodies are the 'temple of the Holy Spirit' (1 Corinthians 6:19–20) and therefore to be used with care. And he advocates that physical exercise is of some value, though training in godliness is much more valuable (1 Timothy 4:8). So the body is certainly not to be despised. But neither is it to be exalted.

Jesus teaches that it is purity of heart, not purity of body, that leads to experiencing God. The heart, in the understanding of Jesus, was the seat of the entire personality. The heart was the motivating centre, the wellspring, the determinative source of life's attitudes and actions. Knowing God then is going to occur when we focus on the heart rather than the body, even though we do not despise the latter. If we want to experience God we must give the same concern, attention, regard, discipline and care to the heart as the good athlete gives to the body. We must exercise spiritually with the same determination with which others are wont to exercise physically.

The moment we look inwardly with any degree of integrity, we will discover that the heart is anything but pure. Knowing what is in our hearts is more than likely to lead us to agree with Jesus when he remarked that 'out of the heart come evil thoughts, murder, adultery, sexual immorality, theft, false testimony, slander. These,' he added, 'are what make you "unclean"' (Matthew 15:19–20). Furthermore, we will quickly discover, if we have not already done so, that attempts to clean up our hearts ourselves are going to prove futile. The task is beyond our capabilities. We need help from outside to clean us up, and help from beyond to keep us clean once we are. The great promises of cleansing in the Old Testament – like that of Zechariah 13:1, 'On that day a fountain will be opened to the house of David and the inhabitants of Jerusalem, to cleanse them from sin and impurity' – came to fulfilment in Jesus. He is the one who is able to clean us up from the inside. The cleansing agent he uses is the blood he shed on his cross (1 John 1:7–9). And he can keep us clean as his Holy Spirit takes up residence in our hearts; that is, in the deepest structures of our lives.

Blessed are the dominant versus blessed are the meek

Nike's philosophy is that competitors need to stare down their opponents, give no quarter, show no mercy and dominate their opposition. Adversaries must be eliminated rigorously if victory is to be experienced. Success goes to the strong, to those who never yield or submit. Weakness must never be shown, for that is to court defeat. Only those who demonstrate such unpitying ruthlessness of attitude will stand on the winner's rostrum and inherit the medal.

Jesus, in complete contradiction to this, taught that it was the meek who would be the champions and inherit the earth. Few would regard meekness as a virtue today. But then few regarded it as a virtue in the ancient world when Jesus first spoke these words. Most considered it a vice, just as most do in our own day. So we're in no different a position than the first disciples. Part of our problem with our understanding of meekness is that we equate it with weakness, and none of us relishes the thought of being a doormat for others to trample over. In fact, meekness and weakness are not the same thing at all. If anything, the Bible's understanding of meekness connects it more with strength than a lack of strength. But meekness is strength that has been controlled. It's strength that directs its energies so that its power is used to serve the interests of others rather than destroy them, to build them up rather than put them down. In the ancient world they often used the word to describe a horse that had been broken in. The horse still had its native power but, through the process of training, that power was now channelled to constructive ends.

One cannot be meek and live the Nike way, making sure that number one always triumphs. One can only be meek by putting the interests of others first.

Philip Yancey wrote in *What's So Amazing About Grace?*,

From nursery school onward we are taught how to succeed in the world of ungrace. The early bird gets the worm. No pain, no gain. There is no such thing as a free lunch. Demand your rights. Get what you pay for. I know these rules because I live by them. I work for what I earn; I like to win; I insist on my rights. I want people to get what they deserve – nothing more, nothing less.[17]

That underlies much of the Nike philosophy. But it is a despairing philosophy, for if we want to live in the world of ungrace and treat others in that way we are likely to

---

17 Philip Yancey, *What's So Amazing About Grace?* (Zondervan, 1997), p. 64.

experience no grace from others in our own lives. And what we need is a grace that comes from above, from God himself, who accepts us just as we are and smothers us in his love, forgiving our sins, cleaning out the filth of our lives, replenishing our spiritually bankrupt accounts with his riches and giving us a power we do not have in ourselves to live differently and live in companionship with him.

Nike says: pick your spirituality from the *à la carte* menu. Find your own way to heaven. Choose your own beliefs. Shape your own morality. All the time it is offering us choice, it is, in reality, preaching a subtle message that points us in one direction. It offers a totally horizontal spirituality that never encourages us to look beyond ourselves and our bodies. It tells us our hope is within us; that our salvation is to do with our bodies.

But Jesus is the man from outside who came to show us God and reveal to us his way. He did not come to leave us wallowing in uncertainty, to negotiate our own way to heaven in ignorance, but to shed light on the one way to heaven. He came to reveal God's truth, which turns out to be strikingly contrary to the spirit of his own day, and ours. He came to make the connection between God and us, through the weakness of the cross, and to be himself the road to heaven. He came to do what we could not.

This Jesus is no mythical figure belonging to the pantheon of imagined Greek deities, who expresses symbolically a hoped-for victory. He is a real historical human being who lived in space and time. He has a date in history. And yet for all his humanness he was also simultaneously totally divine. He came to give us the certainty of victory. He delivered the victory by defeating our enemies on his cross. He delivered the certainty because his cross was not the final act of his life. His life ended not in the defeat of Calvary but the triumph of his resurrection to a new body. His empty tomb is the evidence we need. Victory is assured.

By all means buy the shoes and sport the swoosh on your shirt. But don't be taken in by the spirit of Nike. Do not build on the flimsy foundation of 'Just do it!', for one day it will inevitably fail. Build life on the strong and surer foundation of what Jesus did for us. It's not 'Just do it!' but 'Jesus did it!' – that's the slogan that counts.

2.

Magic Kingdom or Jesus' Kingdom?

When Patricia Gearing buried her daughter in a cemetery near Mablethorpe, Lincolnshire, in 1998 she placed a simple cross on her grave. Local council officials told her she had to remove it, since 'crosses are discouraged'. In its place she asked permission to erect a headstone featuring Mickey Mouse and was told that the authorities would be happy with that.[1] The magic kingdom of Disney exercises a pervasive influence in our society. Its symbols even have the power to displace the traditional symbols of the Christian religion.

The growth of the Disney empire began in 1923 when Walt Disney and his brother formed a company to make cartoons. Not long afterwards Mickey Mouse joined the company and has been one of their most lovable and recognisable characters ever since. Disney's creative genius was attached to a charismatic personality, which meant he was easily able to gather others around him and enthuse

---

1 *The Times*, 6 June 1998.

them with his visions. Business-wise the great break-through came when the first full-length animated feature film of *Snow White* was produced in the late 1930s. From there, in spite of periods of troubled labour history, the Disney empire has gone on expanding, incorporating in its orbit videos, TV, theatre productions, educational pro-grammes, publications, art, collector's items and a whole variety of merchandise. Much later in the day came the theme parks, with the original Disneyland opening in 1955. Later still came the holiday resorts, the cruise lines and the communities of the future.

From small beginnings the Disney Corporation has grown to a mega and multifaceted business that shapes our values on a global scale. In 1994 an estimated $14 billion worth of Disney products were sold around the world. Five years earlier it could already be claimed that 70 per cent of Americans had visited either Disneyland or Disney World. On 24 June 1998 they received their 600 millionth visitor to Disney World. The total empire had assets of $43.6 billion, with a revenue of $23.4 billion. Their 13 hotels and other accommodation offer a choice of 19,502 rooms. Florida became *the* holiday destination for the British throughout most of the 1990s. And while the up-front target market is children, the truth is that adults visiting a Disney theme park outnumber children by four to one.[2]

The Disney theme park, which is the consummate expres-sion of Disney's worldview, has become a place of pilgrim-age, a sacred centre in which children and adults alike enter a

---

2 The information here is based on Janet Wasko, *Understanding Disney: The Manufacture of Fantasy* (Polity, 2001). See especially pp. 33, 49, 75–6, 162–3.

fantasy world where the real world is suspended. On the surface Disney offers a wonderful opportunity to escape from the pressures of our mundane lives, at least for a brief time, and to experience freedom from the constraints imposed on us by the need to work. Not far below the surface it is preaching at us a set of values that is shaping our thinking, determining our lifestyle and moulding our worldview. Disney is much more than a mere producer of entertainment.

The kingdom of Disney

Cultural analysts who have examined Disney portray it as a purveyor of a set of values that includes those of individualism, the work ethic, optimism, escape, fantasy, magic, imagination, innocence, romance, happiness and the triumph of good over evil. In a nutshell these are the values of mainstream America. They derive their power from the creation of a nostalgic past while spurring visitors and customers on to an optimistic future.[3]

The world of fantasy

If one were forced to say in a single phrase what Disney stands for it would be: the manufacture of fantasy. At the heart of the Disney empire lies the Magic Kingdom, which erupts into our more ordinary world in Los Angeles, Orlando, Paris and Tokyo. As one enters the Magic Kingdom, adult and child alike are relieved of their cares, ordinary judgements are put into suspense and a false world, one that exists nowhere in reality, is created. It's a

---

3 *ibid.*, p. 114 and Alan Bryman, *Disney and His Worlds* (Routledge, 1995).

world of colour, of music, of fairy tales (and of queues, but more of that later). It takes one into a world where all is nice, pleasurable and good. It disarms the most sceptical of adults (as I know from my personal experience) and prises open their imagination. Everything, of course, is carefully stage managed. Nothing is left to chance. Not for nothing is the research and development arm of Disney called 'Imagineering'.[4]

The theme park presents the visitor with a complete world of make-believe. Disney, as David Lyon explains, is escapism to a safe and sanitised world where right always triumphs.[5] The triumph of good over evil is a vital component. Children get along with each other through the singing of endless songs in 'It's a Small World' without ever falling out. Mickey Mouse and other celebrities hold audiences. Families can even be photographed with him. The sun perpetually shines, the smiles never dim and the music never stops. If Snow White goes into a deep coma, she will be quickly brought back to life by the kiss of a handsome prince. The monstrous appearance of the Beast can be wonderfully changed by the transforming magic of Beauty's love.

The message of the theme park is distributed beyond its walls through merchandise, film and video. Take *Bambi*, the classic Disney video, as an example. In spite of the tragic shooting of Bambi's mother by a hunter, the blurb on the video jacket is entirely upbeat. It tells us that this is a heart-warming story of a newborn prince of the forest. As Bambi grows he learns to walk, talk and make friends

---

4 Wasko, *Understanding Disney,* p. 59.
5 David Lyon, *Jesus in Disneyland* (Polity, 2000), p. 10.

with other animals like the bashful skunk, ironically named Flower, and a fun-loving rabbit called Thumper. Through it, we're told, we can discover the wonder of life, the beauty of nature and enjoy a wonderful, funny and touching experience. It's a far cry from Tennyson's description of nature as 'red in tooth and claw'. It's not a world where we're bothered with foot and mouth disease or BSE. And, if we are briefly reminded of them, no matter, they are quickly dealt with.

Alan Bryman mentions a publicity leaflet for Disney World which was widely available in British Disney stores and which he justifiably claims is typical. One page described Disney World as 'a wonderland of fun, where fantasies become reality and where reality is fantastic. So let the magic begin.' The next page continued,

It all adds up to a different world with a special kind of holiday magic, unlike anywhere else, and there's always something new and exciting on the horizon. . . *Follow that dream* . . . Don't forget though this is just the beginning of the dream. Wait till you get there, you won't believe your eyes.[6]

A belief in innocence

The perception is that Disney is for children and that children are innocent. Words that describe the world created by Disney would be words like 'joyful', 'positive', 'guilt-free', 'romantic', 'sweet', 'inoffensive', 'safe', 'pure', 'wholesome' and 'virgin'. In doing this Disney may justly be accused of having an over-sentimental view of childhood,

6 Alan Bryman, 'Theme parks and McDonaldization', in Barry Smart (ed.) *Resisting McDonaldization* (Sage, 1999), p. 110.

perhaps by way of reaction to Walt's own. Much of the Disney empire recreates rural America and an idealised past. Here children make a wonderfully smooth transition into adulthood, even if they cannot depend on Mum and Dad to give them the support they might have a right to expect. Many of Disney's characters have lost their parents somewhere along the road, or are separated from them, or they just don't figure in the story. But through their own inner strength the innocent children are transformed into wonderfully well-adjusted adults.

In constructing this world Disney not only provides a safe environment while one is visiting a theme park or enjoying a video, but sends out the signal that this is what the world is (or should be) like. This is not a world where children murder other children, hurl stones at police officers, torture animals for fun, shoplift, disobey their parents, nor even say bluntly rude and embarrassing things to one another. Original sin has been banished, original goodness restored.

When challenged on this, Walt Disney first pointed out that he did not make films just for children. Adults too are caught up in the make-believe world. And then he added, 'The worst of us is not without innocence, although buried deeply it might be. In my work I want to speak to that innocence.'[7] Good though his motivation may have been, his achievement was, in the words of Janet Wasko, to create a world 'which somehow seems foreign to the world in which we actually live'.[8] Perhaps he believed that in creating this parallel universe, innocence would be brought to

---

7 Quoted in Wasko, *Understanding Disney,* p. 118.
8 *ibid.*

the surface and people would be released into niceness. The means of salvation, if such there is, lies in escapism from the real world, by observing an ideal world and imitating the inhabitants of an imagined world.

The experience of emotions

Disney is out to provide its customers with exciting sensations. The visual sensations are stunning, as colour and form collude to transport people to a different world. They stretch the imagination, often fooling the eye and taking people to the very edge of their sensory limits. You can never quite believe what you see. Statues move, walls dissolve, people leap out of television screens, distances deceive. Real world and virtual world collide. What you see around you is constantly and cleverly manipulated. The aural sensations are just as stunning. You are never out of the sound of music, which subtly crafts the chosen atmosphere and moves you happily along to the next stage. Both sight and sound unite powerfully in the daily parade down Main Street, which recreates one or another of the latest Disney epics, like *The Lion King* or *Pocahontas*.

The physical sensations are just as awesome. In Space Mountain you feel you're falling uncontrollably through space, even though the ride is highly controlled and the wall just a metre away from you. In the 360-degree surround cinema you feel that you are in the middle of a stampede as the theatre vibrates, the noise mounts and cattle charge at you, and through you, from many angles. It's panic-inducing, heart-stopping stuff.

An American psychiatrist called Ronald Dahl took his nine-year-old son to a theme park a couple of years ago and went on one of the world's fastest rollercoasters. When they came off his son pronounced his verdict: it was a bit of a letdown. *The Sunday Times* reported:

> His son's life, Dahl realised, was moving at such speed – hanging onto the coat-tails of stressed adults while at the same time taking on board daily a raft of technological and sensory stimuli unknown a generation ago – that he lacked the capacity for emotional acceleration. In other words, nothing gave him a 'speed rush' any more: *he was already coasting at close to maximum.*[9]

Dahl believes that 'sensory overload' is one of the main factors in contributing to the malaise many young people feel in contemporary society. Their boredom threshold is very low. They live on a diet of 'what will excite me next?'. And the level of depression rises.

There's no indication that the theme park to which Ronald Dahl took his son was one of Disney's. But whichever park it was, the cap fits Disney perfectly.

Disney's success in creating a fantasy world and managing emotions to the desired end was ironically revealed in a little incident that occurred at Disneyland in 1995. An armed robbery took place in the car park, which led to a law suit, not against the thieves but against the Disney Corporation. Visitors sued the company because their children had been 'rudely disillusioned'. In responding to the robbery a number of Disney characters gathered backstage and removed part of their costumes, showing themselves to be merely actors after all. The magic vanished. 'The suit alleged that the company exposed the children to "the reality that Disney characters were, in fact, make believe".[10]

---

9 4 January 1998, italics mine.
10 Wasko, *Understanding Disney,* p. 166.

Enough said, except to add that it is not only the visitors whose emotions are successfully managed and manipulated as they are channelled largely into the passive role of an observer. The staff are subject to equal emotional management and are under obligation to exude happiness continuously and never let their smile, nor their politeness, slip. They do not ever look as if they are working, as their primary mandate upon being recruited is to look as if they're having fun.

A commitment to modernity

Underneath all the commitment to fantasy, fun and excitement there lies, on the part of the Disney Corporation, a serious commitment to the culture of modernity. The values that have shaped modern society are the very values that make Disney successful. And those values are subtly preached at the customers in a million little ways.

The business works on strict capitalist lines. At the end of the day what matters is the profit margin. Disney is not mounting a social service aimed at transforming the world. It is about making the bottom line look good.

It maintains its cutting edge in business because it maintains its cutting edge in technology. It has come a long way from the earliest days of making cartoons to the hi-tech productions of today, passing through a number of breakthrough stages in animation and animatronics *en route*. From the intimidating rides to the tiniest toys modern technology is pressed into service. From Disney's own research department, called 'Imagineering', to its business alliances with AT & T, Exxon and General Motors, technology reigns.

Disney has a commitment to the consumerist market. It

has done as much as anyone to homogenise culture so that people from across the social spectrum buy and enjoy its products. It has had a commitment to brand and image second to none. It has broken out of shops only being available in shopping malls and ensured that its goods can be purchased in airports, train stations and at cinemas. It has entered into powerful alliances with other providers of contemporary culture, like McDonald's, to ensure that its products are almost unavoidable, on the basis that possessing one will lead to the desire for another and then another, and that the possession of a toy will whet the appetite for a video, or a visit.[11]

The most important theme of the modern world that one encounters at Disney is the belief in progress. The stage presentations, like the reproduction of Abraham Lincoln delivering his Gettysburg address, preach the rightness of the American way of life, with its belief in democracy and freedom. That is founded on the principle that human beings can transform their own world and infinitely improve it, if only they get the right political structures in place and engineer the right social conditions through education. Elsewhere the belief in progress is even more explicit.

EPCOT stands for the Experimental Prototype Community of Tomorrow. The original vision was that it would be a futurist city in which people would actually live. In practice the project developed differently and no live-in community was formed, though it still exudes confidence in our ability to engineer a future world. The original vision was not, however, forgotten and in 1996

---

11 See Lyon, *Jesus in Disneyland*, p. 5.

Celebration was opened some five miles from Walt Disney World.[12] Here was an actual community where it was hoped 20,000 people would eventually live. It was sold as 'not just a housing development but a community', which would include state-of-the art schools, public space and high speed public transport and would be pedestrian-friendly. Even its weather was to be managed to the extent that 'a massive umbrella would protect its citizens from the rain'. Celebration was brought into existence by using corporate planning to bring the 'lessons of Main Street' to the problems of the suburbs. There is evidence that the experiment has proved a failure. In reality, the residents of Celebration are a highly selective group of white Americans. Other groups exclude themselves or, like the poor and homeless, are excluded. Some residents are already disaffected, and managing tomorrow is not proving quite as easy as Disney might have thought. Nonetheless the confident belief in our ability to engineer progress remains undaunted.

The management of people

In spite of the appearance of exciting commotion, the reality is that most who visit Disney are passive observers in a highly controlled environment rather than active participants. Nothing is left to chance. Shows are highly programmed. Rides are precisely timed. Queues are stage-managed so that visitors are deceived about how long they will have to stand and wait. Strategies are adopted to minimise frustration and impatience. The layout is carefully

12 On the details of Celebration see Wasko, *Understanding Disney*, pp. 178–184.

planned to ensure that you exit through the shop where the goods that will enable you to take a little piece of Disney home with you can be purchased. Disney is the market leader in processing large numbers of people.

People rarely wake up to the true cost of all this, instead becoming eager sacrificial participants in the 'sacred' rituals of the theme park. Bob Garfield of *Advertising Age* once calculated the true cost of a visit to Disney. His family of four stayed in Disney accommodation, ate in Disney restaurants and purchased a five-day pass to the theme parks. Altogether they spent 114 hours on Disney property. But out of those 114 hours they only spent an actual 6 hours 47 minutes on rides or at shows. They spent a huge amount of the rest of the time queuing. Garfield calculated that the real cost was $261 per fun hour.[13]

The kingdom of Jesus

Disney's romantic interpretations of the past and optimistic predictions of the future are designed to make people escape in the present. But once the visit has been made, the video watched or the merchandise purchased, today's reality has an ugly habit of aggressively reasserting itself. The magic wears off. The truth is that nothing has changed. How different is the kingdom of Jesus.

The kingdom of Jesus confronts reality

The very first announcement Jesus made when he began his public ministry was, 'The time has come. The kingdom

---

13 Quoted in Bryman, 'Theme parks and McDonaldization', p. 110.

of God is near' (Mark 1:15). In the person of Jesus, God was dramatically stepping back into the world he had made to rescue it from the control of Satan, who had illegitimately usurped his rule as the rightful king of creation. In order to advance his unlawful designs Satan had sometimes used outright force to bring people into subjection, sometimes he had used cunning deception and sometimes he had just relied on their spiritual indifference. But whatever his strategy the result was everywhere to be seen. The dominion of darkness (Colossians 1:13) over which Satan presided had brought the world to the brink of ruin and incarcerated people in the dankest of prisons. His fingerprints were all over their lives.

Jesus encountered Satan's handiwork everywhere he turned. Look at his activity during a few days Jesus spent either side of the lake of Galilee as Mark 4:35–5:43 records it. Four different incidents illustrate what happens when the kingdom of Jesus confronts the kingdom of Satan.

First, as Jesus and his disciples cross over the lake one evening the boat is almost wrecked and their lives almost lost as 'a furious squall' rises. We need not think that Satan was deliberately out to target Jesus and do away with him before God's appointed hour, although that may be true. Natural disasters frequently occur, bringing death and grief to many and terror to even more. God creates and it is good. Satan destroys and it is terrifying. Human sin does not result in only men and women being out of sync with God; creation itself is out of joint with him as well.

While modern men and women may in some ways be cushioned against the full impact of natural disasters, we have seen enough (and been taken by surprise too many times) to believe that we can control our natural environment. For ancient men and women who lived in a much more precarious world, fear was a daily fact of life and much of their religious practice, among Jews as well as Gentiles, was designed to placate evil and ward off misfortune.

Jesus shared their hazardous experiences. When the disciples cried in fear of their lives as the waves threatened to swamp their boat, Jesus was there in the boat with them.

Second, in the area on the east side of the lake, Jesus and his disciples encounter a demon-possessed man. Every detail of Mark's sharply perceptive account is significant. It shows us what demons can do to wreck a human life. The man lived in the graveyard, more at home among the dead than the living. The self-destructive powers that lived inside him were too great for any human beings to deal with. The normal means of restraint, let alone cure, were totally ineffective in his case. Driven away from his family and cast out of normal community, this man whose personality was disintegrating was a constant suicide threat. Yet the demonic powers within him soon recognise Jesus as the 'Son of the Most High God' and know that their time is up. At his command they leave the poor man alone, enter a herd of pigs and rush over the abyss to a watery grave.

The third incident occurs while Jesus is on his way to the fourth. Back on the other side of the lake, a synagogue ruler asks Jesus to heal his daughter. But before he can do so Jesus stops to interrogate the crowd because he is aware that someone in the crowd has touched him and derived healing from him. It is understandable that his disciples think he's gone barmy at this point. Of course people had touched him. They were in the middle of a mob. Loads of people had done so. But Jesus persists. One person had touched him in such a way that 'power had gone out from him'.

Soon a timid woman steps forward and collapses at his feet. This woman had suffered from an illness for twelve years, had spent all her money on useless cures and now, more in desperation than hope, had come to see if Jesus could make her well. Given the nature of her illness it was no wonder that she did not wish to advertise her presence in the crowd. According to the Jewish law she was unclean and should never have been there contaminating others. But Jesus rewards her faith, heals her and tells her, 'Go in peace and be freed from your suffering.'

Finally Jesus makes it to Jairus's home. But alas, or so they all think, too late. By the time he arrives, Jairus's daughter is already dead. Having encountered a natural disaster, demons and disease, Jesus now encounters Satan's ultimate weapon and our final enemy: death itself. No matter. Ignoring their scepticism at his claim that she is only asleep, and ejecting the mourners from the room, he instructs the twelve-year-old girl to get up, which she promptly does and walks around.

The fingerprints of Satan are seen in the demonic, diseased and death-riddled world that Jesus encounters. They still are. But unlike the magic kingdom of Disney, Jesus never creates a make-believe world where these things do not exist. He never invites people to enter an escapist world where we simply pretend that the harsh realities of life do not matter. He goes right into the thick of all the ugliness and pain of our lives and meets it head on.

The kingdom of Jesus transforms reality

Jesus not only encountered evil in these incidents but genuinely overcame it. He did more than merely express sympathy with those who were suffering because the world was such an awful place to live in. That might have temporarily picked them up and made them feel good for a while, just like a visit to Disney, but it would not have ultimately changed anything. He took action that effected a genuine change in their situation. The storm was calmed and the disaster averted. The demons were expelled and the man restored. The disease was cured and the woman made whole. Death was defeated and the girl brought back to life.

What is more, the changes that took place could stand up to examination. They were not the imagined miracles of some cheap faith healer. The disciples lived to provide an eyewitness account of what happened on the lake of Galilee that night. The man delivered from demons was sent back home to his family and village. They'd know the genuine from the fake. The woman took her place back in the community and the mouths of the cynics in Jairus's house were firmly shut. If you can never quite believe anything you see in the magic kingdom of Disney, it is altogether different in the kingdom of Jesus. His wonders are authentic.

The kingdom of Jesus embraces reality

How does Jesus transform the evil realities of our lives with his salvation? He does so by embracing them on his cross. Jesus is the King who secures his kingdom by his own death. The cross not only secures the forgiveness of

sin but is also the means by which God intends to heal all
the disjointedness of our world, including the natural disasters to which our fallen world is subject. (Romans
8:18–21; Colossians 1:20). Demons met their match on the
cross. There Christ 'disarmed the powers and authorities,
he made a public spectacle of them, triumphing over them
by the cross'. (Colossians 2:15). Our diseases were carried
by him there (Matthew 8:17) and it is by his stripes that we
are healed (Isaiah 53:4–5). Death was embraced there but
could not hold him as he rose from the tomb three days
after his crucifixion (1 Corinthians 15:1–58).

Although each Gospel speaks of Jesus entering into our
suffering and bearing our pain on his cross, it is Mark who
seems particularly to stress it. Mark's account of the crucifixion is stark, and the brevity of his report seems only to
emphasise the awfulness of his execution. Darkness broods
over the account (Mark 15:33). The only cry that gets a
mention is the cry of God-forsakenness (Mark 15:34). To
Mark there can be no doubt that the King in this kingdom
does not remain uninvolved or unaffected by the sin, brokenness, horror and shame of our world. Rather, the King
experiences for himself the dark realities of our lives as he
suffers the abuse of his passion and disgrace of his cross.
There he lets the powers of the world and the demonic
authorities in our cosmos do their worst and submits to
death. But in doing so he overcomes it all and opens up a
new way, a new possibility, transforming the darkness into
light.

It was necessary that he did so, for he would have been
unable to change the situation by staying remote from it in
heaven. Tom Smail puts it well when he writes:

Christ comes to the cross as the fireman comes to the fire, as the lifeboat comes to the sinking ship, as the rescue team comes to the wounded man in the alpine snow. They have what it takes to help and deliver, but they must come to where the fire burns, the storm rages, the avalanche entombs and make themselves vulnerable to the danger that such a coming involves. So Christ on the cross comes to where the Father in his holy wrath has handed over the sinners to the consequences of their sin.[14]

How different from the escapist make-believe of Disney.

So what?

Disney has some positive things to teach the church. God made our world to be a world of colour, music and joy. Too often the church is grey, drab and joyless. Disney brings out the expressive/childlike aspects of our nature. Too often the church worships God only with its mind and not with its emotions. Too often the church is strictly adults only, with little room for children. Disney aims at excellence, and usually succeeds. Too often the church is amateur and fails to reflect the precision and excellence of the God who created our wonderful world.

For all the positive lessons that Disney can teach us, however, there are at least four areas where the church has been infiltrated by the Disney spirit to its detriment.

---

14 Tom Smail, *Once and for All* (Darton, Longman & Todd, 1998), p. 106.

We need to be honest in our struggles

Disney creates a world in which people leave their problems, suffering and failures at the gate and escape into fantasy. It is not a kingdom where honesty is encouraged or reality confronted. Many find the church to be just as unreal a community. People seem so nice and problem-free, especially when they wear their Sunday smiles and Sunday best. Real issues like lust or doubt are never voiced, let alone faced. When some brave soul dares to be honest, for once, his or her cry is quickly suppressed by some over-spiritual fellow believer or, just as often, some embarrassed older believer who is running away from their own vulnerability. The community formed by the King of truth should strive to be a model of integrity. That means we must let people express their failings, their doubts, their stuggles and their temptations. It means being real, not creating fantasy-land.

We need to be real in our worship

The most blatant expression of our lack of reality is seen in our worship. These days the sound of praise is frequently hyped so as to drown out all counter-voices. Anguish and anger alike are stifled by the repetition of yet one more song. The healing balm of worship songs is administered in ever larger doses until the congregation feel good about themselves and about God. Little instruction is given as to why God is worthy of our praise. The act of compulsory praise, like the act of compulsory enjoyment at Disney, is considered in itself to be sufficient. As Oliver Barclay comments, 'songs are thought of more as a way of self-expression than of praising God for one or more of the very good reasons that we have for praise, [so] they . . . reinforce the subjective and human trend of our culture and fail to help much in the long run.'[15]

How different is the worship of the Bible. In the full diet of God-centred worship, advocated and illustrated in Scripture, there is room for silence in the face of mystery, confession in the face of sin, lament in the face of tragedy, and anger in the face of injustice. Consider the way in which most lectionaries have censored the Bible so that none of the nasty angry bits remain. Those who don't use a lectionary are in no better position, resorting frequently to using a very narrow range of the biblical text, which only expresses the narrow, and usually the feel-good, ambitions of the preacher.

Walter Brueggemann, an Old Testament scholar, has argued convincingly that the psalms of lament are vital for us in worship today, just as they were for the Jews. We need them, he writes, as 'a corrective to the euphoric, celebrative notions of faith that romantically pretend that life is sweetness and joy, even delight'[16] – in other words, the Disney version of the Christian life. There is a hurtful side to life we need to bring into the presence of God. Our removing the psalms of lament, and even more the psalms of righteous anger, from our worship testifies, Brueggemann says, 'to the alienation between the Bible and the church'.[17] Since the Bible deals with the whole of life and provides us

---

15 Oliver Barclay, *Evangelicalism in Britain, 1935–1995: A personal sketch* (IVP, 1997), p. 116.

16 Walter Brueggemann, in Patrick Miller (ed.), *The Psalms and the Life of Faith* (Fortress Press, 1995), p. 68.

17 *ibid.*, p. 84.

with tools to express the diversity of our experience before God, we are foolish to retreat into some make-believe world that doesn't really exist, except at Disney.

We must be expectant in our faith

Disney has no power to heal broken lives, yet millions put their faith in the temporary palliative that the magic kingdom can offer. Jesus has the power to heal broken lives and has demonstrated in abundance down the centuries his ability to do so. Yet we are reticent to commend him to our hurting world. Real authority over sin, sickness and Satan belongs to Jesus the King. Ours is a powerful and transforming gospel. But few stand with Paul in confessing, 'I am not ashamed of the gospel, because it is the power of God for the salvation of everyone who believes' (Romans 1:16). Our silences and our actions conspire to demonstrate that as a church we frequently lack confidence in the gospel, with the result that we appear to be ashamed of it.

We must be confident in our future

Disney confidently predicts what the future will be like and seeks to blaze the trail by building the communities of tomorrow. It is a future we can build and whose success is heavily dependent on political solutions and technological advances. Both of these are areas in which it is right for Christians to make a contribution. But our confidence in the new tomorrow depends on neither us nor them. Our confidence is in the new tomorrow that Jesus Christ will bring about when he returns to earth to complete the work he began during his first visit. The kingdom he inaugurated then, which is already in existence but not yet fully realised, will be consummated on his return.

The New Testament uses a vast variety of imagery to speak of this future, for it stretches the human imagination beyond its normal limits. We find it hard to think that one day we will be resurrected from the grave (1 Corinthians 15:12–57), caught up with him in the sky (1 Thessalonians 4:17), part of the new heaven and the new earth (2 Peter 3:11–13), citizens of the heavenly Jerusalem, where sin, pain and tears have been permanently excluded and God reigns among his people, all in all (Revelation 21:1–22:5). But unlike the imagination Walt Disney requires in order for us to envisage his utopia, here is imagination that is solidly grounded on the historic acts of God. He is the one who brought the world into existence and made it good. He is the one who led his people out of Egypt in the Exodus. He is the one who made David's empire great. He is the one who sent us Jesus and, when death thought it had finally disposed of him, brought him back to life again, to live and reign eternally. It is his future to which we must look forward.

Disney does a wonderful service in providing entertainment and escapism for millions of hard-pressed people who live in our world. But at the end of the day it changes nothing. Mickey Mouse cannot save. He's a wonderful mascot if you want fun. He's a lousy master if you seek transformation. The church must always be on its guard lest it adopts the 'spirit of the age', which, in our case, may well take the form of the Disney spirit. We dare not build our communities or construct our worship on the flimsy foundations of fantasy but on the solid foundations of faith in the risen Lord, who entered the muck and pain of our world, brought about transformation in people's lives through his royal power and dealt with what was wrong once and for all by embracing it on his cross.

Who would choose a magic kingdom when you can choose the real kingdom of Jesus?

3.

Fast-Food Junkies or Gourmet Connoisseurs?

When missionaries from South Africa recently visited Bradford and asked children to draw a picture of the cross, one child produced a collage of a McDonald's Golden M and a hamburger.[1] Some $20,000 million has been spent in promoting McDonald's in the last 20 years, which arguably has resulted in the Golden Arches of McDonald's overtaking the cross of Christ as one of the most widely recognised symbols in the world.[2]

Mac and Dick McDonald first opened a restaurant in Pasadena, California, in 1937. Their aim was to produce low price meals at a high speed and in large numbers. To do that they introduced a limited menu and the principles of the assembly line into the food industry. Chefs did not oversee the production of a complete meal. Rather there were 'grill men', 'fries men', 'shakes men' and 'dressers'. By

---

1 *The Sunday Times*, 1 July 2001.
2 Barry Smart, in Barry Smart (ed.), *Resisting McDonaldization* (Sage, 1999), p. 14.

1954 they had a single drive-in McDonald's in San Bernardino, California, which was much celebrated locally. But that was the most sensational thing they had achieved. It was not until that year when Ray Kroc visited McDonald's that McDonald's as we know it today came into being. For a few years he worked in partnership with the McDonald brothers, franchising their name and product. By 1961 he had bought them out and the rest, as they say, is history.[3]

From the single franchised restaurant Ray Kroc opened in Des Laines, Illinois, in 1955, which took $366 on its first day, McDonald's has grown to be a worldwide business with a global impact on culture. Its financial reports for the millennium year, 2000, disclose that it owned 29,000 restaurants, operated in 120 countries, served 45 million customers a day, added 1,606 new outlets with plans to do the same again the following year, introduced 103 new dessert-only kiosks and had a balance sheet of $40 billion.[4] Huge publicity attended the opening of a McDonald's restaurant in Pushkin Square, Moscow, in 1990, resulting in the biggest ever number of customers at any McDonald's restaurant on the opening day. But since then they have added a further 62 outlets in Russia and more quietly expanded their empire elsewhere. In 2000 they opened new outlets in American Samoa and French Guiana without anyone noticing. It has become a fact of our globalised world.

Its vision statement is to offer its customers 'the world's

3 George Ritzer, *The McDonaldization of Society* (Pine Forge Press, 1996), pp. 30–1. See also http://www.mcdonalds.com

4 http://www.mcdonalds.com/corporate/press/financial/2001

best quick service restaurant experience'- 'experience', note, not meal! It aims to be the best employer, to deliver operational excellence and to achieve enduring profitable growth.

The key features of McDonaldisation

Our interest, however, is not so much in McDonald's as a restaurant or a business but as a cultural phenomenon. McDonald's has come to symbolise a way of doing things in any number of areas, not just food production. 'Mc' has become a readily understood prefix when attached, for example, to education and health care. Society has been widely McDonaldised. George Ritzer, Professor of Sociology at the University of Maryland, whose book sparked a widespread debate, defines McDonaldisation as: 'The process by which the principles of the fast-food restaurant are coming to dominate more and more sectors of American society as well as the rest of the world.'[5] Certainly more than America is affected. So just what are these principles of which he speaks?

Ritzer identifies four principles, implies there might well be a fifth and widely illustrates their impact on sports, entertainment, housing, education, health, home cooking, birth and death. Others have investigated their application to even more aspects of life.[6]

Before listing the principles, it ought to be said that Ritzer is not so naïve as to believe that McDonald's invented them. They were at work long before the first McDonald's

---

5 Ritzer, *The McDonaldization of Society*, p. 1.
6 See Smart (ed.), *Resisting McDonaldization*.

restaurant hit the scene. Max Weber, one of the founding fathers of sociology, was fascinated with the underlying issues a century ago. He saw that Western society was becoming increasingly rational in its working and bureaucratic in its methods, and feared that in the end it would lead people to experience life as if they were living in an iron cage.[7] Ritzer acknowledges this and also points to two powerful historical examples that demonstrate the principles at work; one obscene and the other we take for granted, or rather we did so until very recently.

The first is the Nazi Holocaust, which Zygmunt Bauman argues 'may serve as a paradigm for bureaucratic rationality'.[8] The Holocaust was an efficient and rational means of eliminating Jews in vast numbers in a predictable way and in the shortest possible time. It was totally dehumanising but an excellent example of bureaucratic rationality of the most appalling kind at work.

The second example, and a much less emotive one, is the production of Ford motor cars on an assembly line. The same principles of rational bureaucratic organisation devoting themselves to the efficient, calculable and predictable production of a car are apparent. Until recently we would have thought this was the best way to produce a car, but of late questions have been asked as to whether it does not take the rational principle too far and end up being counter-productive because it is too dehumanising. Consequently, some car manufacturers have rediscovered the value of the less 'efficient' team concept that requires

---

7   Max Weber, *The Protestant Ethic and the Spirit of Capitalism* (Routledge, 1930), p. 181.

8   Cited in Ritzer, *The McDonaldization of Society*, p. 22.

people to produce a complete vehicle rather than a single component, but which restores the pride of the craftsman to his or her work.

Be that as it may, the principles of work that McDonald's employs, and employs brilliantly, in the fast-food area are copied widely today in the areas of production, service and commerce. So much so that they affect the way we think in other areas of our life as well.

Efficiency

The first principle Ritzer identifies is that of efficiency.[9] To achieve this, out go temperamental cooks and varied menus. In come production-line assistants with a very limited menu. Every step in the process of producing a hamburger and fries is streamlined. The ultimate example is seen in the Burger King conveyor belt, where a frozen hamburger will be placed at one end only to emerge fully cooked at the other end 94 seconds later. Staff perform a limited number of inflexibly choreographed operations. Touch-screen tills either order the meal or run up the bill, sometimes both. Knives and forks are largely eliminated, and food is prepared so it's easy to eat with fingers or even while driving a car. Customers are encouraged to clear their own rubbish, so fewer staff have to be employed, and there is no washing-up to be done. Drive-in windows are carefully laid out to encourage fewer people to eat in the restaurant itself and more customers to flow through than would otherwise be the case. Car parking is efficiently planned. Space is maximised and, in recent years, smaller restaurants have been planned so as to avoid unfilled seats.

9 Ritzer, *The McDonaldization of Society*, pp. 34–58.

Everything spells efficiency.

This same principle, which, as we have seen, has long been evident in the workplace, is now making its mark in education and health care. Everything is now carefully costed with league tables galore measuring the efficiency of one school or hospital against another. Marking individually written students' scripts is very expensive on time. Why do that when a multiple choice questionnaire means they can be marked much more quickly and more objectively as well? In some cases a computer is able to do it for you, dispensing with costly teachers altogether. No matter that the student may not understand as much! Hospitals are measured for their through-put of operations, maximisation of bed usage, success of treatment and fatality rates. The less efficient are held up to public ridicule as wasters of community resources at best, and dangerous at worst. Even crematoria operators join in the game. Their magazine periodically lists them in league tables according to their efficient use of gas and the time taken to dispose of bodies. In a world where McDonald's reigns it seems as if nothing is sacred.

Calculability

The second principle is that of calculability.[10] There is no possibility that the size of bun you get at McDonald's will vary. A random quantity of fries will never be served. To quote Ritzer,

> . . . great care is taken to be sure that each raw McDonald's
> hamburger weighs 1.6 ounces, no more, no less; there are ten

---

10 *ibid.*, pp. 59–78.

hamburgers to a pound of meat. The precooked hamburger measures precisely 3.875 inches in diameter, the bun exactly 3.5 inches. McDonald's invented the 'fatilyzer' to ensure that its regular hamburger meat had no more than 19% fat.[11]

The cheese, the onions, the number of McNuggets, the cooking process are all just as carefully calculated.

Quantity matters at McDonald's, or so it would have you believe. You are never offered a small drink. The smallest on offer is a medium one, while the largest is super size. You are never offered a small hamburger, but you are encouraged to order a Big Mac and large fries or a Bacon McDouble with cheese. For just a few pence extra your ordinary meal can be turned into an Extra Value Meal. The implication is that you'd be foolish not to.

Again, it takes little imagination to see the same principle at work in other areas like education and health. One official famously got into trouble not so long ago for referring to residents in care homes as 'income-generating units' rather than as people, and for voicing the need to maximise bed occupancy by clearing out the dead quickly, in order to get funds to make ends meet. People were no longer people. They were calculable units of finance.

Predictability

The third principle is that of predictability.[12] For those who travel the world, predictability is one of the blessings McDonald's has to offer. Whether you're in Argentina or Austria, Jamaica or Jerusalem, Rio or Russia, Singapore

---

11 *ibid.*, p. 63.
12 *ibid.*, pp. 79–99.

or Saudi Arabia you have the confidence that the menu on offer and the food produced will be the same. You know what you will get. There are, of course, some local variations. I can recall my astonishment in going to one McDonald's in Virginia where they did not serve milkshakes and my delight in going to another in Norway where I enjoyed a salmonburger. But the variations are strictly limited and make only the tiniest dent in the façade of predictability one generally faces.

The service customers receive should be as predictable as the food they eat. Customers entering the restaurant are about to take part in a ritual that is almost as carefully scripted as any religious liturgy. It's planned to cover all the main issues that will arise in the very limited conversation that will ensue. It begins with greeting the customer, and proceeds through taking the order, checking the order, assembling the order, presenting the order and receiving payment for the order, and concludes with blessing the customer with the words 'have a nice day'. The easiest thing to do to create chaos at McDonald's is to engage the assistant in conversation, treat them as a real person and ask them how they are. To do so is to fracture the magic liturgy – and take up unnecessary time.

Once again, Ritzer argues, the wider world exhibits this principle at work. Perhaps the explosion of population has made mass production and mass delivery inevitable. If so, it has certainly had a widespread effect. Education, for example, is no longer devoted to bringing out the full potential of individual students but to processing them *en masse* through the machine that turns out look-alike graduates. Ritzer calls it 'cookie-cutter' education, relying on 'cookie-cutter' texts. But it is perhaps the leisure industry that exhibits the principle most. Theme parks are highly controlled environments that minimise to the point of oblivion anything unforeseen happening and produce predetermined doses of happiness for its visitors.

Control

This fourth principle relates to the way in which organisations have increasingly come to control people through the use of technology.[13] Ritzer's apocalyptic vision is that 'once people are controlled, it is possible to begin reducing their behaviour to a series of machinelike actions. And once people behave like machines, they can be replaced with actual machines such as robots.'[14] As yet, we haven't reached this stage. But eating in McDonald's is still a highly controlled experience. People move through the process as if they, not the hamburgers, were on a conveyor belt. They stand in line, choose and order, carry their meal to the table, eat, remove their litter and leave. Subtle mechanisms are in place to prevent people from lingering at their tables too long. It is even claimed that some fast-food restaurants have designed their chairs to make sure customers feel uncomfortable after 20 minutes.[15]

Reacting to just this production-line way of consuming food, one Italian Catholic theologian recently urged Roman Catholics to spurn the hamburger as a Protestant food. His reasoning was that eating food was a sacred and communal experience for Catholics over which there should be time to linger. 'People go to McDonald's,' he

13 Ritzer, *The McDonaldization of Society*, pp. 101–20.
14 *ibid.*, p. 101.
15 *ibid.*, p. 106.

said, 'in search of the quickest possible meal. The aim is to bolt down food and satisfy hunger as quickly as possible in order to devote themselves to other things.' But in doing so they were displaying the Protestant work ethic, being 'unCatholic, perhaps even atheist', and paying for it in 'obesity, stress and other ills of modern urban life'.[16]

From the numerous vending machines that dispense snacks and drinks, through the machines that yield only reluctantly if we can produce exactly the right coins or ticket at the exit of a car park, via the uncomprehending voice-data answering machines that instruct us, in less than human tones, to enter 3 on our phones, followed by the hash, *we are controlled*. While the same may not be quite as apparent in education or health, the trends are unmistakably there. Much of our leisure is technologically controlled, with the machines on which we're exercising switching off after we've used them for the stipulated amount of time, or the court on which we're playing being occupied by someone else after the paid-for hours, regardless of where we are in the game we are playing.

A fifth principle?

Ritzer gets close to saying that wherever the above principles are put into practice a fifth principle nearly always comes into play. It is this: 'Rational systems inevitably spawn a series of irrationalities that limit, eventually compromise, and perhaps even undermine their rationality.'[17] You see it in a McDonald's restaurant in the queuing in which the customers engage. Drive-in McDonald's are

---

16 *The Times*, 10 November 2000.
17 Ritzer, *The McDonaldization of Society*, p. 121.

even worse, as they compel cars to snake their way around the building using up fuel and polluting the atmosphere while their drivers wait for their precious hamburgers. The prices look good, but, truth to tell, healthier meals could be produced cheaper at home. Disposable containers mean we save on the washing-up but at the irrational cost of producing more rubbish than the planet can cope with. There is an argument, too, that such a system discourages creativity and results in low productivity. The experience of one family visiting Disney, mentioned in Chapter 2, is another example of how we're all seduced into behaving irrationally. Supermarkets do it to us all the time. We want just a loaf of bread or a pint of milk, but it takes a strong-minded shopper to come away with only that. We are forced to wind our way through endless miles of aisles offering multitudes of commodities we do not want and end up either buying what we had not intended or wasting more time than we've got. So much for efficiency!

The same is true in many public services and in education. In the interests of doing things properly and recording the evidence in such a way that it cannot be controverted in a court of law, police have little time to catch criminals since they spend their time filling in forms. In the interests of objectivity, double marking has been imposed in most universities since the primary marker may be biased. For us at LBC, this has meant that students no longer receive their work back as quickly as they once did (which it has always been argued is key to the learning experience) and that by the time it has been through the 'system' the student has lost all interest in what they submitted and no longer learns anything from it. As long as the process is being served, the objective can wait. The question is no longer whether students have learned anything, and still less whether they have become anything, but whether the correct procedure has been followed.[18]

It seems that the McDonald's experience is not quite so rational and efficient after all.

McDonaldisation and the church

While the idea of the McDonaldisation of society is not without its critics,[19] George Ritzer has put his finger on something that at a popular level provides us with a key to understanding what sort of world we live in. None of us lives in a vacuum, and McDonaldisation, as with the other cultural icons and metaphors this book explores, affects our lives in a variety of ways. It certainly leaves its mark on the way we practise our Christian faith. So, what is the impact of McDonaldisation on those of us who are believers in Jesus Christ? A couple of writers have begun to explore the answer to that question, but after looking at what they have said I want to develop the issue in a different way.

McDonaldisation and evangelism

As far as I know, the first person to apply the idea of McDonaldisation to the church was Peter Ward, then the Archbishop of Canterbury's youth officer, in a provocative article in the *Church Times* about Alpha.[20] Alpha, he argued,

---

18 John Drane, *The McDonaldization of the Church* (Darton, Longman & Todd, 2000), p. 30.
19 For which see Smart (ed.), *Resisting McDonaldization*.
20 *Church Times*, 8 January 1999.

was a process composed of prepackaged simple steps that provided a national brand and label anyone could franchise. It took a 'frozen non-Christian' and cooked them with the gospel until they emerged at the other end of the process as a fully committed believer. Alpha's fascination with numbers, evident in all their publicity, smacked of the preoccupation of McDonald's with quantity. It offered a predictable experience for people so that the uncertainties of those undertaking a course were minimised, wherever they did it. While it used little non-human technology, it was a fairly controlled process, with Nicky Gumbel's videos being the mainstay of an Alpha evening, and the training manuals and books provided by Alpha telling local presenters how to handle matters and answer the questions raised.

In writing like this, Peter Ward was not trying to be cynical. Indeed, he gladly affirmed that God was at work through Alpha. And he believed there are good things we can learn from McDonald's. Even so, he believed that a cultural analysis of the process was helpful and could alert us to some important spiritual questions, such as whether it did not lead to a uniform and somewhat superficial version of the faith, or whether it gave sufficient room for a sovereignly free Holy Spirit to work in ways other than those planned. 'McDonaldisation,' he concluded, 'is not by any means all bad, but it should not be baptised uncritically.'

In a reply to Ward, Sandy Millar, the vicar of Holy Trinity Brompton, the home of Alpha, protested that the only similarity between McDonald's and Alpha was 'the desire to get the product out to as many people as possible'.[21] But perhaps he should not have been so defensive.

The significant thing is that Alpha is only the last of a long line of approaches to evangelism that have packaged the gospel in easy steps and franchised it to others. It is a well-worn evangelical technique arising from our roots in the Enlightenment, which had a commitment to systematise everything. Billy Graham's training of counsellors, Bill Bright's *Four Spiritual Laws*, James Kennedy's *Evangelism Explosion* and even Norman Warren's *Journey into Life* have been adopting this approach for years.[22] So have thousands of evangelical preachers who have talked about the ABC of the gospel. The plus factor of Alpha is that by recognising that evangelism is a process and structuring the programme around meals and weekends away it has taken the relationship factor more seriously than most previous techniques.

Whatever the conclusion regarding Alpha might be, Peter Ward raises some important issues. Granted that we can benefit from McDonald's in seeking to be as zealous for the gospel as it is about hamburgers, and that the church does need to ask the sort of questions about strategy and efficiency McDonald's asks, there are also some cautions. Evangelism isn't marketing, and making disciples isn't the same as producing hamburgers. If Jesus is our model, we need to take seriously that:

- Evangelism needs to be incarnational. Jesus lived among people, shared their lives, entered into their pain and bore their burdens.

---

22 See James Davison Hunter, *American Evangelicalism: Conservative Religion and the Quandary of Modernity* (Rutgers University Press, 1983), pp. 73–84.

- Evangelism needs to be personal. Jesus had no set formula to which everyone had to assent. He dealt with the Pharisee, Nicodemus; the woman at the well in Samaria; and the sick man at the pool of Bethesda very differently.[23] The first needed to be born again, the second to drink a draught of life-giving water and the third to get up and walk. He met each one of them at their particular point of need and expressed the good news in ways that were applicable to them.

- Evangelism isn't about counting heads.[24] There were times when Jesus was forsaken by the crowds (John 6:60–66) and when potential disciples seem to have been discouraged rather than enlisted (Mark 10:17–23). It is about making disciples who, for all they have to learn, are genuine.

McDonaldisation and worship

More recently John Drane has written a wider assessment of the impact of McDonaldisation on the church. He reflects from a different angle on the way it influences our evangelism, and spells out his conviction that the church doesn't know enough about the people it is trying to win for Christ and is misguided to treat everyone the same, whereas in fact they are all very different.[25] Some of the

---

23 The incidents are found in John 3–5.

24 Having said that I do believe that God's normal plan for the church, as demonstrated in the Acts of the Apostles, is that it should grow. Caution needs to be exercised in too glibly opposing quality and quantity.

25 Drane, *The McDonaldization of the Church*, pp. 55–84. He identifies the desperate poor, hedonists, traditionalists, spiritual searchers, corporate achievers, secularists and the apathetic.

groups he identifies, particularly those of a more hedonistic, arty or seeker disposition, will never be reached by a McDonald's approach to evangelism. Radical changes are called for.

But Drane's major concern relates to the McDonaldisation of worship.[26] Nowhere are the characteristics of efficiency, predictability, calculability and order more evident than here. In our use of space, repetition of liturgy, commitment to words, elevation of the minister or preacher, and rejection of the creative use of emotions and arts we have reduced what is meant to be a living encounter between God and the whole of our beings, including our bodies and emotions, to an activity that just relates to our minds. Drane's special ire is reserved for the way the church celebrates the sacraments. In one tradition they use individual cups with tiny cubes of bread and in another tradition they use bread that 'tastes like disks of soft plastic'.[27] He would be even more horrified at the product I have on my desk as I write. It consists of a disposable individual communion cup, already filled with wine, which has a disk of bread sealed in its lid. It certainly makes for an efficient distribution of bread and wine at communion, but is surely a commitment to efficiency, predictability and calculability gone mad. Drane pleads for a release of imagination, of movement, of drama, of mime, of the visual and of the prophetic in worship. Worship must address the whole person and cater not only for those who are left-brained but for those who are right-brained as well.

The verdict John Drane passes on contemporary wor-

---

26 See *ibid.*, pp. 85–111.
27 *ibid.*, p. 96.

ship is that not only are the children of believers disillusioned by worship and leaving the church in droves but
that

> . . . huge numbers of regular adult worshippers also seem
> bored out of their minds by what goes on in a typical service.
> All of this raises a crucial question, for if worship does not
> 'work' for large numbers of those who regularly participate in
> the life of the Church, not only is that going to sap our own
> spiritual vitality, but it will ensure that we have little confi-
> dence in inviting others to join us.[28]

John Drane has drawn attention to issues of vital importance for the survival of the church. Huge numbers are
leaving it and the way worship is conducted is a factor in
this. The church is often too small, too confined, to cater
for the growth of different personalities in their spiritual
pilgrimage.[29] Whether all Drane's proposals for change are
either workable or the ultimate solution is another matter.
He has rightly highlighted the deficiency of a McDonald's
diet when it comes to worship.

Like John Drane, I too fear that much contemporary
worship sets a McDonald's-type meal in front of people,
but I fear it for very different reasons from him. Much
contemporary worship seems to me like fast food because
it sets meagre fare in front of people rather than the varied

---

28 *ibid.*, p. 86.
29 An excellent research project on those who have left evangelical,
   charismatic and Pentecostal churches in New Zealand substantiates
   the point and deters us from claiming that those who leave lack
   commitment or perseverance. See Alan Jamieson, *A Churchless Faith*
   (Philip Garside Publishing, 2000).

menu of worship to be found in Scripture. Two ingredients dominate: the singing of endless but 'sound-bite' worship songs, and the expression of a desire to enter more fully into God's presence – a desire that never seems to be fulfilled. How much more varied is biblical worship, containing elements of mystery, adoration, penitence, lament, anger, intercession and proclamation, as we mentioned earlier. Older hymns, which I realise now belong to a musical genre that is past, had a number of merits. They were able to cater for a range of emotions, experiences, phases and seasons in the Christian life. And they were able to develop and explore Christian truth beyond the superficial. They also tended to major on proclaiming, with confidence and gratitude, what God has accomplished for us in Christ rather than merely expressing the yearning of our own hearts, although some did that beautifully too. For example, they did not spend time expressing the desire to enter 'behind the curtain' into the presence of God. They proclaimed that Christ's death had ripped the curtain in two and made it our right to enter by faith.

Contemporary worship often appears to be designed to generate an existential experience; a feel-good type of relationship with one another and with God. It plainly shares two of the characteristics of McDonaldisation. Much of it has become as predictable as a McDonald's meal. We mercifully no longer indulge in the hymn–prayer sandwich, but we now string several songs together with little or nothing in between them and call it 'a time of worship'. It's different, but just as predictable as worship ever was. And it is just as controlled as it was in the days of one-man ministry, only now it is controlled by music and 'the worship band'.

McDonaldisation and spirituality

Recognising the importance of both the above attempts (evangelism and worship) to relate McDonald's to the church, my own concern would be somewhat different. I am concerned about our McDonaldisation of personal spirituality.

When the characteristics of McDonald's are spelled out, one thing is frequently unspoken but often implied: a concern about the quality of the food produced. A McDonald's meal is quickly purchased and consumed. It is conveniently packaged so that it is manageable. A whole English breakfast, of sorts, can be found wrapped in one bun. It is served in dimensions that can be picked up in the hand, or, like Chicken McNuggets, in bite-sized portions. The calorie-filled, salt-encrusted and sugar-coated meal is, at least to me, immediately satisfying to the taste buds. It's designed to make me feel good and want more. And it succeeds! But is it nutritious? Is it good for me? Does it provide me with a balanced diet? Would I continue to be healthy if it were my sole diet?

To these questions the nutritionists have, over the years, answered with a resounding 'no'. One went so far as to rename the McDonald's burger McClog the Artery. Undoubtedly some of the critics have been alarmist. But equally without doubt some of the criticisms have been valid, otherwise McDonald's itself would not have been so proactive in seeking to change its practices to take them into account.[30]

---

30 For details see Ritzer, *The McDonaldization of Society*, pp. 129–30.

A McDonald's hamburger has its place in the rich diversity of food on offer in the contemporary world, particularly when there is the need for a quick refuelling stop. But as one's staple diet it would be seriously deficient. Yet many live spiritually on a diet akin to McDonald's hamburgers. They never do more than have a quick refuelling stop with God in which they take in snacks that seem immediately satisfying and make them feel good for a brief time but which are of little value in building strong, healthy disciples. They do no more than engage in spiritual comfort-eating. Older generations of believers spent time studying the Scriptures and cultivating their relationship with God through frequent and lengthy time being spent in his presence. Now we're too busy to do that. Life is too pressurised. If we do it at all (and the evidence from those who produce daily Bible study notes is that fewer and fewer of us are doing it) we only manage to take in a bite-sized portion of the Bible. We don't get the grand sweep of Scripture or understand its depth and wonder. We just grab a mouthful of a verse or two, which will serve as a motto for the day or provide us with some therapeutic warmth as we go to face the real world. Often we're doing it on the run. The reading and praying is done on the bus on the way to work (which is certainly better than not doing it at all), while we are surrounded by distractions and unable to take too much in.

What is more, we're often more concerned about the packaging than whether the content is of any value. Unless the Bible is presented in magazine form, or in some other visually stimulating way, or mediated through song, we don't want to know. My point is not that any of these means of communication are wrong. I welcome the diversifying of the means of communication and the use of the visual as well as the verbal. My point is that so often, as Marshall McLuhen taught us, the medium is the message. We must be very careful therefore to get behind the medium and ask whether it is delivering anything worthwhile. We must teach ourselves to judge the value of something not by whether it interests us or grabs our attention, but by whether or not it is right.

Just before a lecture one morning one of my students was rejoicing that he had managed to read a whole chapter in a book earlier that week. It was obviously a new experience for him. I was trying to be encouraging and made the mistake of asking what the book was. It was one of the many exciting but ill-founded, even semi-heretical, books that have been published in recent years. When I asked what he thought of it I was disturbed to be told it was great and 'felt right'. As yet this student, warmly commended by his local church as a gifted leader among their young people, had not developed any ability to evaluate books from a biblical viewpoint. It had not occurred to him to ask whether what the book was teaching was soundly based in Scripture or not. His spiritual taste buds had been trained to enjoy fast food – and only fast food. He needed to be introduced to a more nourishing diet. Like many of his generation, he had been fed a spiritual cuisine that was superficial in the extreme.

The result of this is that the place of Scripture has been devalued in some public worship and often little attention is given either to reading or to teaching it. Sometimes it is not read at all or read in a poor and cursory manner. Where it is read, it is often no more than the mere preface to a sermon. It does not address us in its own right; it merely serves as a launching pad for the preacher, whose address often has little to do with biblical revelation. I've been to a number of services where Scripture has not actually been used at all. But I am sure everyone present thought it had been. They would have protested their evangelical fidelity while denying their evangelical credentials by the practice of their worship. It is quite different from the sort of advice Paul gave to Timothy in 1 Timothy 4:13: 'Until I come, devote yourself to the public reading of Scripture, to preaching and to teaching.'

By contrast, preaching today is judged by whether it succeeds in capturing our interest or not. Never mind the question of truth.

The same is true, to a significant extent, of Christian service. Exciting short-term opportunities exist which are often tied in with leisure opportunities and presented as if they are real training for Christian service. The model of the big platform entertainer is most visible. Immediate rewards are sought and whether people enjoyed themselves is the measure of success. We do the rising generation of Christian leaders a grave disservice if we do not level with them about the realities of serving Christ. For all the joy of it, and it is joyful, there are the long hidden periods of preparation and practice, the arduous hours, the times of monotony and struggle, the learning from the failures and the need to be as spiritually authentic and conscientious behind the scenes as well as when on the platform and stage. It's not as easy as being a 'grill man' and producing a hamburger. And if we tell them it is we tell them a lie. No wonder so many give up too soon and drop out in disillusion. Christian workers need to be much more like a well-trained chef who is able to produce a gourmet meal. Paul, whose writing about his own struggles and joys in ministry was never anything but honest, used the image of being careful about what materials one used when building the house of God and warned of the need to check out whether we are using 'gold, silver, costly stones, wood, hay or straw', especially if we want our work to survive divine inspection (1 Corinthians 3:12–13). I wonder if today he might have contrasted the fast food that many are producing with the gastronomic feasts that should be produced.

An image of the Christian life is being projected that is not unlike a McDonald's meal. Instant and appetising in the short term, it is cheap and easy comfort-eating. But the trouble with fast food is that it breeds a generation of junkies whose palates have never been developed and whose taste buds do not know there is something more delicious and nutritious available. We need to move people beyond fast-food spirituality and train them to become gourmet connoisseurs in their relationship with God. This is not because of some desire to be elitist. Rather it is because it is within the grasp of all to enjoy the full flavour of the gospel and because God has designed us for a healthier, more mature and more appetising spiritual diet. McDonald's may be great for kids, but grown-ups deserve something better.

When David had sinned against God and sought to repair the relationship with him by building an altar on which to offer a sacrifice, Araunah, who owned the site on which the altar was to be built, offered the land to him for free. David replied, 'No, I insist on paying you for it. I will not sacrifice to the Lord my God burnt offerings that cost me nothing' (2 Samuel 24:24). Now the connection with McDonald's has nothing to do with burnt offerings. In their efficient and highly controlled environment burnt offerings never occur! But it does have to do with cost. McSpirituality costs us little, if anything. The spirituality God desires will cost much. It will lead us to walk the way of the cross with Christ. It will drive us to the limits of our resources so that we might depend on him. It will turn us outwards from a preoccupation with self and feelings. It will change our characters from the inside out. But it will be worth every penny. And it will enable us not only to be more satisfied with God ourselves, but to set decent spiritual food before a spiritually famished world.

4.

Consumers or Disciples?

The broadcaster John Humphrys believes that Napoleon got it wrong. 'We are,' he writes, 'no longer a nation of shopkeepers, we are a nation of shoppers . . . Shopping is what we believe in.'[1]

Saturday afternoons used to be a bore. Our family never indulged in the pleasure of a premier league football match. For us Saturday afternoon meant the weekly shop. Bundled into the car, we'd make our way to the nearby small market town where we'd traipse around in what felt like a never-ending tedious ritual of popping in and out of the multitude of tiny High Street stores. The drudgery was only relieved by the purchase of a delicious chocolate bar from the half dozen or so to choose from in Woolworths. The men (or boys), of course, protested more than the women. For them, at least, shopping was a chore.

How things have changed. What used to be arch-enemy number one has now become leisure choice number one.

---

1 John Humphrys, *Devil's Advocate* (Arrow Books, 2000), pp. 103–4.

For the vast majority shopping has transformed itself into a pleasure. The tiny High Street stores have given way to the enticing Aladdin's cave of the shopping mall, often removed from the High Street, where warmth and colour seductively envelop the consumer. The mall self-consciously boasts 'the food court' and multiplex cinema, which serves to underline the message that the boundary between buying and leisure is entirely artificial. It has become so pleasurable, in fact, that shopping is even seen as a means of healing. We speak of it as 'retail therapy'.

Equally shopping has become an act full of religious significance. The architecture of the shopping mall often imitates the older architecture of the village church, complete with clock and steeple, revealing its true identity. The shopping mall, as has often been pointed out, is the temple where the consumers practise their religious rituals (until the Internet takes over, if it ever does) and bow down before the idols of fashion displayed in the various shrines of the market economy.

What's happened to bring about this transformation? What effect does it have in shaping our thinking? How should Christians respond?

One expert observer claims, with little fear of contradiction that, 'Our society is a consumer society.'[2] By that he means more than just that we all buy things. People always have. From earliest times people have engaged in some form of exchange of goods, and commercial activity is nothing new. But now the whole of our society and culture is shaped by merchandising, branding, advertising and

2 Zygmunt Bauman, *Globalization: The Human Consequences* (Polity, 1998), p. 79.

consuming. This was made possible in the twentieth century because of advanced mass production techniques, foreshadowed by Henry Ford in the car industry, being combined with creative marketing techniques that made use of the new media of radio and TV. It turned us all into consumers.[3] Full employment and surplus cash meant we had the resources to become consumers. Consuming was no longer what we did; it was about what we had become.[4] Hence the frequently quoted adage *Tesco ergo sum*[5] ('I shop therefore I am') has replaced the older Enlightenment understanding of what forms our identity, summed up in Descartes' phrase *Cogito ergo sum* ('I think therefore I am').

As Craig Bartholomew points out, we need to distinguish between commerce and consumer*ism*.[6] Consumerism was inherent in the logic of the modern industrialised and capitalist world. It is commerce taken to its illogical conclusion, for it makes us purchase things we do not need. It is commerce cheapened, for it leads us to know 'the price of everything and the value of nothing'. It is commerce run

---

3 Andrew Walker, *Telling the Story: Gospel, Mission and Culture* (SPCK, 1996), p. 143, and Craig Bartholomew, 'Christ and Consumerism: an introduction' in Craig Bartholomew and Thorsten Moritz (eds), *Christ and Consumerism: A critical analysis of the spirit of the age* (Paternoster, 2000), p. 5.
4 See Jean Baudrillard, *The Consumer Society* (Sage, 1998).
5 'Tesco' is not to my knowledge originally a Latin verb but could well have been an appropriate one for 'I shop' had the Romans so decided. I attribute the phrase *Tesco ergo sum* first to Lesslie Newbigin. 'Tesco' is, I believe, a shortened form of 'Tessa's Company' and is derived from the name of the founder's daughter.
6 Bartholomew and Moritz (eds), *Christ and Consumerism*, p. 6.

riot, for we become its slave rather than it submitting to us as masters.[7]

The Bible and material possessions[8]

The distinction between commerce and consumerism is helpful, not least in helping us to understand what the Bible teaches about material possessions and in helping us relate it to the world in which we live. The Bible often seems to celebrate material prosperity in a way that causes many of us to blush (unless we've bought into the distorted and unwarranted so-called gospel of prosperity) since we have heard materialism denounced so often from the pulpit as a heinous sin. Yet the Lord is the one who brags that 'every animal of the forest is mine, and the cattle on a thousand hills' (Psalm 50:10). And his glory is served by 'the wealth of the nations' being brought as gifts to the restored Jerusalem (Isaiah 60, especially verse 11). How does this fit?

Four elements of the Bible's teaching in this area may help:

- We need to see all we have as a gift from God rather than as something we have a right to possess. Again

---

7 See Richard Foster's related comment, 'We must clearly understand that the lust for affluence in contemporary society is psychotic.' *Celebration of Discipline* (Hodder & Stoughton, 1980), p. 70.

8 An excellent practical introduction to the issue can be found in Richard Foster, *Money, Sex and Power: The Challenge to a Disciplined Life* (Hodder & Stoughton, 1985). A more serious biblical theology can be found in Craig Blomberg, *Neither Poverty nor Riches* (IVP, 1999).

and again the children of Israel were taught that the land they entered and possessed was not theirs but a gift of God, literally a land inherited because of his promise rather than because they had a right to it (for example, Deuteronomy 8:10–18). In the New Testament Paul echoes the same principle in asking the arrogant Corinthians what it is they have that they did not receive as a gift (1 Corinthians 4:7).

- We need to avoid idolatry at all times: the idolatry of absolutising and worshipping things made by human hands. To do so is logically absurd (since we made them) and spiritually destructive (Isaiah 46:5–10; Jeremiah 10:1–16).

- We need, even in the midst of celebrating God's goodness to us, to remember the poor. Apart from the wider biblical teaching about care for the poor, the issue is brought into sharp focus in Nehemiah 8:10, where God's repentant people are told not to mope and mourn in an ungrateful fashion but 'Go and enjoy choice food and sweet drinks, *and send some to those who have nothing prepared*.' It is right to celebrate God's bountiful provision, which is his creation intention for all men and women, but not to do so in such a way that it becomes an exercise in social irresponsibility and self-indulgence.

- We need to receive everything with deliberate and spoken thanksgiving to God (1 Timothy 4:4–5). The exercise of this spiritual discipline will save us from arrogance, deliver us from a 'rights' mentality and make us grateful and generous, as opposed to a grasping and greedy, people. We need to verbalise our thanks to God through, for example, the saying of grace before a meal,

in some other act of prayer or by consciously remind-
ing each other of God's blessing on us. If we never
express our thankfulness, but only ever pause silently
for a moment, we are likely soon to take its expression
for granted and then before long we shall stop being
thankful altogether.

Consumerism and contemporary society

Our concern in this chapter, however, is more with a
Christian's attitude to consumerism than a Christian's attitude to material possessions. Consumerism affects much
more than our shopping habits. It affects the way we live
life on a much broader canvas than that. The consumer
mentality has become deeply ingrained as a way of seeing
the world and now touches almost every aspect of our
social and working lives.

Consumerism says that everything can be 'commodified'

In a consumerist society we produce, market, sell and buy
'commodities'. Commodities are simply things we trade.
When we used the word in the past we applied it to things
like washing machines, cars, fridges and TVs. They were
tangible goods that had been manufactured and then sold
on to us through a retail outlet of some sort. But now
everything is seen as a commodity. Health, education, services, law and order, culture and even religion have become
commodified.

The impact of the consumer mentality has been
extremely visible in the health service. Doctors have
become fundholders, and beds in hospitals have to be 'purchased'. When one health authority has sold its stock of

particular medical or surgical procedures, negotiations have to be entered into with others to see if they can supply them. The culture is one of managerial contracts rather than the covenanted service that used to characterise nurses, doctors and hospitals. Productive efficiency is measured not only so that the costs can be calculated exactly but so that the customers can see the relative value and efficiency of a particular health authority by seeing where they come in the league tables.

It's the same across the board. Take literary culture as another example. That too has become commodified. The classic novels of Jane Austen or Thomas Hardy continue in circulation because they can be abridged and packaged for television. When the series is on, or the film is released, the sales of the books go up. They are not commended as elevating to the mind, still less to the spirit, but as a racy story or a scandalous adventure. They are presented not for their own sakes but to ensure that the TV channel wins the ratings war it perpetually wages against its rivals. Culture therefore becomes accessible to all, but only at the expense of being a matter of consumer choice and purchasable just like a kettle or a mobile phone.

The church is just as vulnerable to the forces of consumerism as anyone else. But more of that later.

Consumerism says that everything must be marketed

If everything is capable of being reduced to a commodity, we can see then that the logic is that it must be marketed. Stiff competition means that advertising becomes more and more frenetic and reaches into areas that hitherto have been advertising-free zones. No longer does electricity simply arrive in our house from the one public supplier, but we're bombarded by gas companies who want to sell us cheaper electricity than the electricity industry can itself. The phone company uses the phone more than the customers do to convince us that we can't do without that unique special offer that is available only to its 3 million most favoured customers. The universities tout for business by advertising for students in local bus stations because they need to widen access to higher education and attract those who previously would never have thought of studying for a degree. Numbers need to be kept up so that government grants can be obtained and good positions secured in the league tables *vis à vis* their competitors.

In addition to the marketing of literary culture, we have already seen that the connection between culture and commerce is even more evident at the popular end of the market. Take the alliance between the empires of Disney and McDonald's, which is potent. No film stands on its own. No cartoon or children's programme takes place in isolation. No Disney animation is just for entertainment. It's about business – about the business of getting people to watch it at the cinema *and* buy the hamburger, and then the toys, the clothes, the books, the watches, the stationery, the videos, the DVDs, the umbrellas and the trinkets, which continue to proclaim its message. They all reinforce each other. The sale of one item leads to the sale of a range of items.

It's the same with the church. From Coca-Cola to cars, from classics to clergy, they all have to be marketed. If we've not yet reached the point, unlike leaders in politics, where bishops are elected primarily for their media skills and telegenic personalities, we're not far off. Everything must be marketed.

The values and effects of consumerism

Consumerism is not a neutral fact of contemporary life; it is one that powerfully configures our mindset. It carries within it values that are all the more dangerous because we take them for granted. Let's think about five of the most significant issues consumerism throws up.

Consumerism is self-centred

When I go to the supermarket *I* am a powerful person for *I* am a consumer. That puts me at the centre of every transaction. If I don't find the brand name of something I want on the shelves, in the size I want, at the price I want, I'll shop somewhere else. If I find what I want, in the right quantity and at the right price, I will buy it. It is not quite right to say that customer choice dictates all, because there are other more hidden forces (the forces of marketing and fashion) at work. We are not quite the free human beings we like to think we are. Even so, we are powerful. Ask Dorling Kindersley! When customers said 'no' and refused to buy the quantities of *Star Wars* books they had produced, they made huge losses and had to sell the company. Ask the great food chains why they're so concerned about 'customer services' and reduced check-out queues. It's because the customer is 'prince', if not 'king', in a consumer society. And the customer measures everything by him or herself – likes, wants, desires, needs, timetable and taste.

Susan White sets out the picture like this:

In the beginning of this narrative is the self-made, self-sufficient human being. At the end of this narrative is the big house, the big car and the expensive clothes. In the middle is the struggle for success, the greed, the getting, the spending in a world where there is no such thing as a free lunch. Most of us have made this so thoroughly 'our story' that we are hardly aware of its influence.[9]

Consumerism exalts choice

A recent survey by Paul Williams of Southampton University discovered that anyone who undertook a serious investigation of all the options available in mobile phones in order to find out which was the very best for them, taking just one minute on each option, would take 150 years to complete it, by which time, presumably, the mobile phone would no longer be of any use to them.[10] This research only highlights the absurd degree of diversity with which we are confronted. We can easily be made punch drunk with choice. Think how many varieties of breakfast cereal or toothpaste call out to us from the supermarket shelves.

Some handle the diversity by refusing to make a choice at all. I did when it came to mobile phones. I didn't have the time or the energy to choose. I refused to have one until my wife gave me one as a birthday present! Most of us, however, see choice as a right we all possess as individuals in an increasingly individualised society. We assume that we ought to be able to choose, to get exactly what we want and when we want it. It is the outworking of a long process of

---

9 Quoted in Bartholomew and Moritz (eds), *Christ and Consumerism*, p. 2.
10 *The Times*, Weekend Money, 4 December 1999.

political democracy and freedom,[11] as well as the advance of technology, which makes an ever-increasing variety of product a viable option.

Long ago Peter Berger and others pointed out that such a wealth of choice leads us to a condition of homelessness. We never belong or settle anywhere. We simply migrate from one position to another, one experience to another, one product to another. 'It goes without saying,' he wrote, 'that this condition is psychologically hard to bear.'[12] And they were writing well before the diversity of choice we now face had accelerated to its present rate. Serious questions are now being asked as to whether the rise in the incidence of depression is not related to having too much choice. If there were no choice about what to buy (or believe) we would buy (or believe) what's put in front of us. But if we can choose, we become anxious as to whether we have chosen (or believed) the right thing, or whether we've wasted our money or energy or commitments on the wrong thing. Hence we get depressed.

Choice is, of course, the luxury of the Western world. Elsewhere it is very different. While we worry every few months about what is the best way to update our computer technology and are confronted by bewildering choice, it remains a fact that the majority of people in the world have still not made a single telephone call! While we puzzle over which of the dozens of breakfast cereals to buy, it is still a fact that thousands die of hunger every day.

---

11 Jonathan Sacks develops this theme in *The Politics of Hope* (Jonathan Cape, 1997), e.g. pp. 115, 176.
12 Peter Berger, Bridgitte Berger and Hansfried Kellner, *The Homeless Mind: Modernisation and Consciousness* (Penguin, 1974), p. 77.

Consumerism becomes addictive

We no longer confine shopping to the necessary chore of obtaining essentials in order to live. Shopping has become something we do regardless of need. Buying has become a compulsive activity – we do it, whether we need what we buy or not. The more we do it the more we want to do it. It is habit-forming and dependency-creating, like a drug that enslaves. We are a nation of shopping junkies. And the advertising industry and the working of our economy conspire to keep our habits fed.

Paul's words to the Corinthians are apt in this situation. Writing about fulfilling sexual desire he first of all quotes their popular slogans and then puts in his own riposte: '"Everything is permissible for me" – but not everything is beneficial. "Everything is permissible for me" – but I will not be mastered by anything' (1 Corinthians 6:12). Christians should be free from all controlling forces in their lives except the perfectly liberating controlling force of Christ.

Consumerism shapes our values

No longer does our society determine our values and then, as a consequence of what we treasure, shape our consumption accordingly. Rather the reverse is true. We first determine what we can sell and then derive our values from our consumption.[13] Hence designer clothes and the fashion industry determine what is the right image, and image is all. We are not schooled to look beyond image to charac-

---

13 I owe this point to Bartholomew, 'Introduction', in Bartholomew and Moritz (eds), *Christ and Consumerism*, p. 6.

ter. Sex is marketable and so sex must be disconnected from any moral framework to do with the commitment of one man and one woman in lifelong marriage. The pressure to remove restrictions on pornography is logical in such a society. If it sells, it must be right. And sell we must, 364 days a year,[14] 7 days a week and (increasingly) 24 hours a day. The deregulation of trading hours betrays our true values. We worship consumerism and no longer value the thought of space – a breather from the ceaseless round of commercial activity – created by the shops being closed. We don't want to preserve space for religious worship, family life or wholesome recreation — factors that used to determine our values – because the value that dictates all is the right to shop.

We judge the rightness of something by whether it sells or not, rather than by any deeper moral principles. Similarly we judge the 'value' (to use the word in a way that stretches it beyond credibility) of entertainment, music, TV programmes and films by where they come in the charts and the ratings tables. If it can sell, people must not be denied it, for that would limit their freedom. So, with few exceptions, freedom to purchase is seen as an inalienable right just as much as the freedom of speech and freedom of religion for which our forebears fought. The exceptions (like selling glue and alcohol to under-18-year-olds) betray something of society's uneasy conscience at the margins, but are not to be taken too seriously. Politicians have recklessly been travelling down the one-way street of deregulating anything in the moral sphere in

---

14 Several stores opened even on Christmas Day in 2000 but are still not permitted to open on Easter Sunday.

recent years, with the result that the state has moved out of all areas of defining value as far as our sexual, family and social lifestyles are concerned, leaving the high priests of consumerism to preach what's right and what's wrong from the pulpit of choice. If ever a pulpit was six feet above contradiction this one is!

Consumerism promises freedom[15]

We've all been fooled. Consumerism has sold us a lie. It tells us that if only we could have the latest fashionable clothes . . . if only we could use the most up-to-date IT system . . . if only we could escape on that Caribbean cruise . . . if only we could own that car . . . then we would have freedom, we would be fulfilled, we would shake off the frustrations of life we currently feel and fill the aching void inside. Of course, it never happens. The addictive nature of consumerism means that when we've bought the latest thing there is something else we desperately want. It's like the Russian doll. We're endlessly opening one layer only to find another underneath and we never get to the end.

In Zygmunt Bauman's words:

If consumption is the measure of a successful life, of happiness and even of human decency, then the lid has been taken off the human desires; no amount of acquisitions and exciting

---

15 See especially Zygmunt Bauman, *Intimations of Postmodernity* (Routledge, 1992), pp. 224–5. Bauman, a leading sociologist, while perceiving consumerism to be 'a very central category' in understanding contemporary society accuses it of 'duplicity' by promising that everyone can be happy if they are free to exercise consumer choice and by pretending that freedom is to be equated with consumerism.

sensations is ever likely to bring satisfaction in the way 'keeping up to the standards' once promised: there are no standards to keep up – the finishing line moves forward together with the runner; the goals keep distant as one tries to reach them. Far ahead, records keep being broken . . . there are no standards except those of *grabbing more*, and no rules, except the imperative of 'playing one's cards right'.[16]

Far from delivering freedom, consumerism is an idolatry that enslaves. The book of Proverbs puts its finger on it when it says,

> The leech has two daughters. 'Give! Give!' they cry. There are three things that are never satisfied, four that never say 'Enough!': the grave, the barren womb, land, which is never satisfied with water, and fire, which never says, 'Enough!' (Proverbs 30:15–16)

Spiritual consumers

The consumerist mentality has made serious inroads into the way we practise our Christian lives. Three examples follow.

Consumerism and our relation with God

We buy into God to the extent that it suits us to do so. We take what we want from him and shop elsewhere for the rest.

No one has articulated our changing view of God more accurately or more passionately than David Wells. He writes of the way in which we no longer view God as one

16 Zygmunt Bauman, *Postmodernity and its Discontents* (Polity, 1997), pp. 40–1.

who is awesome in his sovereignty and whose words we must obey. Instead, he says, our perception of God's greatness has been so diminished that today he is 'weightless'. Two quotations from his book *God in the Wasteland* will suffice:

> We have turned to a God that we can use rather than a God we must obey; we have turned to a God who will fulfil our needs rather than to a God before whom we must surrender our rights to ourselves. He is a God *for* us, for our satisfaction – not because we have learned to think of him this way through Christ but because we have learned to think of him this way through the marketplace. In the marketplace, everything is for us, for our pleasure, for our satisfaction, and we have come to assume that it must be so in the church as well. And so we transform the God of mercy into a God who is at our mercy.

> We will not be able to recover the vision and understanding of God's grandeur until we recover an understanding of ourselves as creatures who have been made to know such grandeur. This must begin with the recovery of the idea that as beings made in God's image, we are fundamentally *moral* beings, not consumers, that the satisfaction of our psychological needs pales in significance when compared with the enduring value of doing what is right. Religious consumers want to have a spirituality for the same reason that they want to drive a stylish and expensive auto. Costly obedience is as foreign to them in matters spiritual as self-denial is in matters material.[17]

From our faulty view of God other consumerist attitudes flow to emaciate our Christian lives.

---

17 David Wells, *God in the Wasteland* (IVP, 1994), pp. 114, 115.

Consumerism and our relation to the Bible

Craig Bartholomew points out how foreign it is for any university Department of Theology to view the Bible as God's word.[18] That has been true for a long time, but in its most recent phase scholars feel the biblical text cannot be said to have a true meaning (even if they subsequently reject it) but only a variety of different interpretations put forward by a plurality of scholars. The marketplace of ideas that clusters around the banner of hermeneutics reduces clarity and certainty, but is one that is positively welcomed by the academy. It means you can make the Bible say what you like and convincingly argue that it says the exact opposite of what it appears to be saying on the surface.

Ordinary Christians (as opposed to academic scholars!) are just as guilty of doing the same, even if they do not use the fancy academic apparatus of intellectuals to justify it. We pick and choose the bits of the Bible that suit us. We read it selectively and interpret it to our own advantage. We ignore the uncomfortable bits or write off those bits that jar with contemporary culture – like forgiving enemies rather than getting even with them, or caring for the poor – by saying the writers were only addressing the first-century church and its culture. We pick and mix the Bible's message just as we do sweets in a confectioners in order to make our reading of it comfortable and ensure that we do

---

18 Craig Bartholomew, 'Consuming God's word: biblical interpretation and consumerism', in Bartholomew and Moritz (eds), *Christ and Consumerism*, pp. 81–99.

not seriously diverge from consumer culture, even in our Christian discipleship.

Consumerism and the church

The most obvious sign of consumerism is seen in the way we 'do' church today. Churches have become shops we visit to satisfy our needs rather than covenant communities to which we belong no matter what. If the church is unable to supply our needs – either in terms of worship style, length of sermon, provision of youth clubs or whatever – then we shop around until we find one that does. The consideration of what churches believe about the way they govern their lives, practise the sacraments, or view themselves in relation to the world (all matters that previous generations held to be the crucial distinctions between one church and another) never crosses our minds.

We pick and choose the limits of our involvement in church to suit ourselves. At church, just as in the supermarket, we are the customers whom the managers have to keep happy. We are the centre of the transaction. So the issue is not simply that we will go to any church that suits us, just for as long as it suits us, but that we will *use* the church rather than *belong* to it.[19] We view it as something *they* do for *us*. So we say, '*They* should run a Sunday school for our children, but we are not prepared to get involved and teach ourselves.' Not a few stand back and criticise from the sidelines that others won't get involved in sharing the leadership of the church, while justifying their own lack of involvement because of the pressure of other work or family responsibilities. This is why, at least in part,

---

19 Rick Warren, *The Purpose Driven Church* (Zondervan, 1995), p. 395.

many churches have been obliged to employ more and more staff, like administrators and youth workers, because they are unable to rely on voluntary help from the members as they once could.[20] Too often we are as much consumers in church on Sundays as we are in the shopping arcade on Saturdays.

Space prevents me from developing another aspect of consumerism: that the church is preoccupied with 'marketing' the gospel. Few see any difference between evangelism and marketing and think purely on a horizontal level, leaving spiritual dynamics out of account altogether and reducing the content of the gospel until it becomes so attractive that the offence of the cross (1 Corinthians 1:18–25) is removed completely.

Consumers or disciples?

As Christians we are called to be disciples of Jesus Christ, not consumers of religion. So we are called to live in a way that stands in profound contradiction to the dominant culture in which we live. A disciple is someone who by definition has a personal attachment to a master that shapes the whole of their life and leaves no doubt as to who is in charge.[21] He, the master, is the centre of the transaction. To be a disciple of Christ means:

---

20 This is not the whole story concerning the growth of employment of church workers. It also has to do with the increasing professionalisation of standards and the growing bureaucratisation of society.
21 See Michael Griffiths, *The Example of Jesus* (Hodder & Stoughton, 1985), p. 43.

- We will follow our Master, without regard to personal cost or popularity, just as the earliest disciples did (Mark 1:17, 20; 2:14; Luke 5:28).
- We will accept his teaching, be it ever so revolutionary, without equivocation. That means not just his teaching on bits we agree with, like sexual ethics, but on our relationship to the poor (see, for example, Luke 14:7–14), or on our style of leadership (Mark 10:42–45), or on not holding grudges (Matthew 5:43–48).
- We will adopt his companions, even if they would not be our personal choice. If they follow him, however imperfectly, they are one with us, as the original disciples had to learn (Mark 9:38–41).
- We will imitate his lifestyle, however counter-cultural that may prove to be. Perhaps it is at the point of living simply[22] that we need to imitate him most (Matthew 8:20). We need to learn afresh that it is in losing our life that we shall gain it (Mark 8:34–38). What does it profit us if we possess all our consumerist world has to offer at the expense of forfeiting a true and deep life with God?

As Christians we should be able to enjoy God's rich creation, and the wonderful things available through human hands as a result, without being seduced by the lie of consumerism. Each generation faces a different challenge as to what it means to be authentic disciples. For our generation a key aspect of the challenge is to shake free from the shackles of consumerism and follow our Master in total and joyful submission.

---

22 For practical help see Richard Foster, *The Freedom of Simplicity* (SPCK, 1981).

5.

Tourists or Pilgrims?

Tourism has come a long way since Thomas Cook introduced the idea of conducted tours and founded the first travel agency. In 1841 he organised a railway trip from Leicester to Loughborough for a temperance meeting, and the first excursion was born. Now the tourist industry has grown to be a huge enterprise composed of almost 2 million employees and 125,000 businesses in the United Kingdom. In 1999 it catered for 33 million holidays abroad in all, 15 million of them packaged holidays by air. In addition it looked after 26 million visitors to Britain as well.[1]

One of the most astute commentators on our culture, Zygmunt Bauman, has argued that tourism is a key metaphor of the way we live.[2] We see life as a journey and

---

1 Statistics derived from *Transport Statistics Great Britain: 2000 Edition* (Department of the Environment, Transport and the Regions).

2 The metaphor is explored in a number of places, most notably in *Globalization: The human consequences* (Polity Press, 1998), pp. 77–102; *Life in Fragments* (Blackwell, 1995), pp. 72–104; *Postmodern Ethics* (Blackwell, 1993), pp. 240–4 and *Postmodernity and its Discontents* (Polity Press, 1997), pp. 83–94.

approach it with the mentality of the tourist. All of us are affected, even if, as we shall see, we never get up out of our armchair and never set foot on a foreign shore. It affects not only what we do with our leisure time but how we approach our work and our families. The tourist mindset is: 'life itself turns into an extended tourist escapade, as the tourist's conduct becomes the mode of life and the tourist's stance becomes the character. . .'[3] It's the way we now live and it contrasts sharply with the way we once lived.

The characteristics of the tourist

In a nutshell, the tourist is a person who travels through other people's territory looking for amusement and excitement. Tourists, of course, pay for the pleasure they derive, and meet at least something towards the cost of satisfying their curiosity. But they, unlike genuine explorers, never seriously want to engage with the people or places they visit. Like the consumer they remain the centre of every transaction, determining where they visit, what and when they eat and even the language they speak.

It's worth paraphrasing Bauman's anatomy of the tourist:[4]

- Tourists never belong to the places they visit. Somehow they contrive to be 'in' the place and yet 'out' of the place, that is distant from it, at the same time.
- They travel as if they are 'enclosed in a bubble', which in some cases, of course, they literally are, in their air-

---

3 Bauman, *Life in Fragments,* p. 97.
4 See Bauman, *Postmodernity and its Discontents,* pp. 89–93.

conditioned coaches from which they only ever briefly alight. In the protective bubble, literal or otherwise, they feel safe. A closer, more genuine or uncontrolled contact with the 'natives' might make them feel insecure.

- They travel lightly, with only just enough to protect themselves against the inclemency of the weather and the inhospitable nature of their alien environments.

- They may be on the road again at a moment's notice. They have no attachments that will make them stay. As soon as they tire of the amusement, or feel threatened, they're off to the next place. 'If it's Wednesday it must be Geneva; if it's Thursday it must be Rome; if it's Friday it must be London.'

- Freedom means the freedom to travel, to be entertained, to find pleasure.

- The point of the tourist's life is to be on the move, not to arrive.

- If any roots are struck, they are shallow. Relations with those who live permanently in the tourist areas are only skin deep. Locals are 'used' or 'bumped into' rather than people with whom one builds lifelong friendships.

- They have no loyalty to their travelling companions. An occasional Christmas card might follow, or even a holiday romance,[5] but neither is likely to last.

- There is no real logic to their itinerary. It's just a series of episodes, with 'not to be continued' written all over them. 'Been there, done that, got the tee shirt.' The

---

5 Research conducted by Mori in 2001 found that three-quarters of all British people were in the market for a holiday romance, although only one in three had had such a fling before. www.mori.com/specarea/travel/case.shtml

tourist never expects to return because there is always somewhere more exciting/exotic to explore.

- They feel in control because they make the choice, and as consumers of travel, choice is all.
- Of course, they pay for it. And the freedom they enjoy is proportional to the price they pay.
- They never belong, but they have paid not to.

Bauman recognises that not everyone is a tourist. Some are vagabonds. They share one thing with tourists: they also pass through other people's spaces without any serious destination in mind. But they are 'involuntary tourists'; tourists, in fact, without money. They move because they have to, not because they choose to. The world is inhospitable to them because they can't pay their way and haven't bought the right to be there.

There are also, Bauman points out, strollers. You find them in shopping malls. They live life on the surface, engaging in a series of fleeting encounters that have neither depth nor impact. They just move, in a defined area, from one fleeting encounter to another. The latest form of stroller is the one who sits in front of the television, surfing the channels courtesy of the remote control. Bauman says, 'The ultimate freedom is screen-directed, lived in the company of surfaces, and called zapping.'[6]

Then there is the player, who sees life as a succession of games in which risks are taken, intuition is exercised and the normal rules of life are suspended for a time. Like children, players are willing to embrace life as if it were a game.

---

6 Bauman, *Life in Fragments*, p. 93.

All of these are related, in one way or another, to the dominant metaphor of contemporary life which is that of the tourist. The world is, Bauman claims, 'a tourist's oyster', there to be lived pleasurably, and it is in the pleasure that the meaning of life is to be found.[7]

The implications of the tourist

If we explore the metaphor of the tourist further we discover that it has several challenging implications for the way we live. Remember, being a tourist is not what we do with our two precious weeks of holiday each year. It is what we have become; what we strive to be all the time.

Tourism and identity

One of the key aspects of being a tourist is the avoidance of being fixed. The tourist lives life spontaneously, fluidly, responding to whims and changing directions and destinations. There is an element of uncertainty to the tourists' lives in which they rejoice (providing, of course, it doesn't go too far and plunge them into unexpected crisis or force them into too close a relationship with the locals). That mindset carries over into the rest of life.

We do not want to be trapped in an identity, a place, relationships or situations from which we cannot escape. We refuse to mortgage our futures. Gone is the pride my grandfather knew when he received his gold watch from the Great Western Railway, having worked for them for 40 years. In its place, people string together a series of occupations and are always on the move to avoid being fixed

---

7 Bauman, *Postmodern Ethics*, p. 241.

and bored. In some cases, to stay too long – say, five years – in a job is considered a sign of a lack of an adventurous spirit and counts against you when looking for a new post. We cut off the present at both ends so that we neither pay respect to the past nor serve as a hostage to the future.[8]

Our identities change in other ways too. A recent report on Jane Fonda spoke of her having reinvented herself as a born-again believer. It pointed out that she had previously found her identity as the 1960s sexpot Barbarella, as an anti-Vietnam war activist and as an aerobics guru before becoming 'a millennial Baptist'.[9] It implied that she was unlikely to maintain her religious identity for long before becoming something else. Life's like that now. We do not construct a solid identity with one chapter of it emerging coherently from another. It consists of a series of discon-nected and sometimes quite radically different identities. We don't settle to anything. Bauman summarises the posi-tion in these two telling quotes:

> The hub of postmodern life strategy is not making identity stand – but the avoidance of being fixed.

> The figure of the tourist is the epitome of such avoidance. Indeed, tourists worth their salt are masters supreme of the art of melting the solids and unfixing the fixed.[10]

Tourism and relationships

The area where we see this at work most clearly is in that of relationships. Like the brief and perfunctory encounters

---

8 Bauman, *Postmodernity and its Discontents*, p. 89.

9 *The Sunday Times*, 22 April 2001.

10 Bauman, *Postmodernity and its Discontents*, p. 89.

the tourist has with the locals, we enter a succession of brief and perfunctory encounters with others. The recent film *Flight Club* summed it up well. Edward Norton is thinking about his life while indulging in an airline meal on a plane journey. It consists of single-serving portions of everything: milk, butter, roll, mini-Coke and the rest. Then he realises his relationships are just like that. Life for him consists of a series of 'single-serving' relationships. The closest he ever gets to people is on the flight itself, hence the name of the film.

While postmodern generations are always crying out for community, those schooled in the culture of modernity look on in total disbelief. Postmodern generations seem to them to go about their search for community in entirely the wrong way. They have a succession of short-term relations, one-night stands that lead nowhere. They treat relationships like flat-pack furniture: easily constructed but always fragile and just as easily dismantled. To enter into any long-term commitment engenders the fear of being trapped. Marriage in particular is seen as a prison from which it is hard to escape. So why get yourself entangled in the first place? Hence a rising number of people are leaving marriage until much later in life than their parents did, if they enter into it at all. Even when they do so, divorce is seen as a fairly routine option and it seems as if reconstituted families will soon be the order of the day.

Tourism and work

According to Bauman, the whole of life is now to be lived pleasurably, and that includes the world of work. He writes:

Tourism is no more something one practises when on holidays. Normal life – if it is to be a good life – ought to be, had better be a continuous holiday . . . Ideally, one would be a tourist everywhere, everyday.[11]

So work should no longer be the grind it once was. Hours should be flexible and dress codes relaxed; the team spirit should be jolly, the boss fun, the goals short term and the rewards great. Computers have removed the drudge factor from employment while simultaneously opening up the world, through the Internet, before our very eyes, allowing us both to experience excitement and to enjoy play without even leaving our desks. The computer delivers the freedom of the tourist to the office.

I can well imagine that some would react to this by saying that Bauman has got it wrong, very wrong. Given the McDonaldisation of the public sector, at least, many have experienced work to be going in the opposite direction. There has never been more regulation to deal with than today, never more targets and league tables, never more measurement of productivity and never more pressure (and paperwork) in medicine, the police, schools and higher education. I have a great deal of sympathy for that criticism of Bauman's position. He certainly has a capacity to overstate the case and be selective in the picture he paints. He writes a lot about the experience of being a tourist, but little, if anything at all, about the experience of being the tour operator. Things are different for them. They, like the employees of Disney, may look as if they are having fun but in practice they are working to a tight set of demands

11 Bauman, *Postmodern Ethics,* p. 243.

laid down by others. This is another side to Bauman's coin, which he ignores.

And yet he has a point – a real point. The old heavy production industries have faded from the scene and in their place have arisen industries based on computer technology which are much more employee-friendly in their way of working. By most measurements the experience of work for most of us is far more pleasant than it used to be. The stuffy old businessmen have given way, along with the bowler hat and the rolled umbrella, to the Richard Bransons of this world, who make it fun. And the ability of many young, unqualified (that is not to say untalented) whizz kids to make mega bucks by taking risks in some virgin sphere where the cautious men of yesteryear, schooled in the Protestant work ethic, would never dare to venture is one of the most unsettling revolutions of our time.

Tourism and morality

'Tourism is bad news for morality.'[12] Tourists may get physically close to foreigners, but they have the luxury of remaining spiritually distant. After all, they've paid for the luxury of freedom from moral duty. As Bauman imaginatively puts it, 'the package-tour kit contains the preventive medicine against pangs of conscience next to pills preventing air sickness'.[13] On the one hand, manifestly unjust practices (such as the enforced use of child labour or child prostitution) can be ignored and explained as local custom – 'That's just the way they do it here. Who am I to

---

12 *ibid.*, p. 242.
13 *ibid.*

interfere?' On the other hand, some local customs (like prostitution or drunkenness) can be indulged in because one is far away from home.[14]

Tourists can live their lives without regard to the long-term effects of their behaviour. Tourism, to give another example, is a major contributor to environmental pollution in at least two respects. First, in using fuel to fly aircraft to transport people to their destinations and, second, in the tons of detergent deposited through the waste disposal systems of hotels due to excessive use of soap and shampoo, and the hotel's requirement to wash sheets and towels daily.[15] But never mind pollution. Tourists are free to enjoy themselves.

Previous generations believed that it was possible to devise moral rules that would be universally applicable. But confidence in doing so has long since gone. In its place we have put the right of the individual to devise their own morality and the key criterion for doing so is no longer whether something is right or wrong but whether it is interesting or not.[16]

Britain's Chief Rabbi, Jonathan Sacks, has developed just this point in a different way in his profound analysis of contemporary society, called *The Politics of Hope*. He points out that while individualism flourished in the nineteenth century, society was held together because individualism went hand in hand with the formation of virtue and the cultivation of moral character. Today the moral framework and commitment to character have been eroded.

---

14 See note 5 above.

15 An increasing number of hotels are waking up to the problem and requesting guests to use towels for more than one day.

16 Bauman, *Life in Fragments*, p. 100.

With the decline in family life, which was the crucible of character – the place where we learned about trust, sympathy, sociability, responsibility, attachment and morality – and, equally, with the decline of those intermediate voluntary associations, like the church, the Boy's Brigade or the Girl Guides, we are left with an unbridled individualism that is destructive of community.[17] We don't realise, he says, what we have done. We have treated our moral landscape as if it were Regent's Park in central London, a space open for all and for the benefit of all, and decided it would be much better to carve it up into little segments for the benefit of those who wanted to buy bits of it. It would, Sacks says, provoke a public outcry. But that is exactly what we have done with our collective morality.[18]

We have not done this without cost. The first price we have paid is that while we have privatised morality, we have nationalised responsibility.[19] So we dare not dictate people's personal, sexual or family lifestyle. People must be free to choose to live how they like. But the state, the government, call it what you will, must pick up the bill if there is a cost to pay. Abortion must be available on demand from the National Health Service for any who have chosen to have sexual relations outside marriage without bothering about the necessary precautions. Divorce can cause untold misery in a child's mental health, but no matter, the social services and counselling agencies will be there to provide the necessary support. Family breakdown can cost the country enormous sums of money, but again, no

---

17 Jonathan Sacks, *The Politics of Hope* (Jonathan Cape, 1997), p. 191.
18 *ibid.*, p. 198f.
19 *ibid.*, p. 132.

matter, people can live how they choose: the state will provide. John Humphrys gives what would be an amusing illustration of this point if it were not so close to the truth. Writing of obese schoolchildren who are sent on special courses to boost their self-esteem, he comments somewhat unsympathetically:

> Boost their self esteem? If they ate fewer chips and burgers they would be less fat and that, presumably, would do the trick. Ah, but that requires discipline, and their parents taking responsibility. Since their parents are probably doing the same thing it is unlikely salvation will lie in that direction. Now – hallelujah and praise the Lord! – we have Xenical. Pop a pill or two and if you eat a greasy burger the fat is not absorbed. Once again we have the drug company telling us this is not a lifestyle drug. It is for those who are clinically obese. Of course, of course. No doubt the company will fight like tigers to stop the pill being sold to those who want to buy it (or have the NHS buy it) so that they may continue their gluttony without piling on the calories.[20]

But if John Humphrys is thinking of mounting a campaign against Xenical and for disciplined eating he should be warned that he is on a losing wicket. In the world of the tourist, we are allowed to eat what we want.

The second cost to which Jonathan Sacks points is the rise of the procedural state. Once the restraint on individualism, which resulted from training in temperance and morality, is removed, anything goes. But no society can survive such unbridled individualism. Since it can no longer depend on people being people of integrity, temperate

---

20 John Humphrys, *Devil's Advocate* (Arrow Books, 2000), p. 47.

in character, modest in their demands and caring towards others, it has to legislate to ensure that we are. Hence the rise of a mass of legislation designed to spell out in minute detail how people should behave. Health and safety legislation, employer's legislation, minimum wages, tenancy agreements, national curricula; you name it and, in recent years, we've defined it – unless, that is, it has to do with lifestyle choice and sexual morality.

Tourism and maps

Tourists need guides, couriers or maps. In past societies there was a collective moral (even spiritual) wisdom that served as the guide. But the world of the tourist has rejected this received wisdom in favour of individuals trying to find their own way. It is a journey of uncharted individualism. Consequently, people turn for direction and help to a whole variety of personally chosen advisers. In place of the traditional pastors and priests of the church there is now a major industry of counsellors, coaches, spiritual directors, personal trainers, astrologers, alternative health experts and gurus from which one can choose. They claim to have superior knowledge or to provide access to a wisdom that is not available to all, with a view to providing personal reassurance on the journey of uncertainty.[21] The truth is, having rejected traditional wisdom, we are travelling without any reliable maps.

So then, while the metaphor may be overplayed and the reality is more complex than Zygmunt Bauman would suggest, he does offer us a major insight into the way many of us have been shaped in our thinking and subconsciously

---

21 Bauman, *Postmodernity and its Discontents*, p. 178.

view the world. His position is well summarised in these words taken from his book on *Postmodern Ethics*:

> Society is there for individuals to seek and find satisfaction for their individual wants. The social space is, primarily, a grazing ground. None allows, nor calls for more moral spacing. The written or unwritten citizen's charter of consumer society underwrites the status of the citizen as a tourist. A tourist always, on holiday and in daily routine. A tourist everywhere, abroad and at home. A tourist in society, a tourist in life – free to do his or her own aesthetic spacing and forgiven the forgetting of the moral one. Life as the tourist's haunt.[22]

The calling to be pilgrims

Christians are by no means immune to the mindset of the tourist. Many of us are literal tourists who enjoy our travels to foreign parts thanks to the local travel agent. The more adventurous of us go to more exotic places, maybe because we think Florida or the Spanish islands will be too boring. The more spiritual of us go on one of the many Christian packaged holidays and justify our indulgences by the fellowship and teaching we enjoy (or endure?) during the trip. In doing so we are buying into the mentality of the tourist and reinforcing it as a valid way of viewing Christian discipleship. Christian or not, the mindset is the same. Even those who hardly travel any distance at all are affected. Just as the smell of cigarette smoke lingers on our clothes when we have been in the company of smokers, even if we never smoke ourselves, so we pick up the odour of tourism and are impregnated with it. It affects

---

22 Bauman, *Postmodern Ethics*, p. 244.

our ordinary lives and it affects our spiritual lives.

Perhaps the best way to understand its spiritual implications is to contrast the metaphor of the tourist with the biblical and historic metaphor of the pilgrim. Both the tourist and the pilgrim are on a journey, but there the similarity stops. How different is the ethos of pilgrimage from that of tourism. God calls us to the former, but not to the latter. We should be very careful that we do not forsake the one for the other.

Consider the nature of pilgrimage.

Pilgrims respond to an invitation

When Abraham set out from Ur of the Chaldeans it was in response to the call of God (Genesis 11:31–12:9). He may not have known the precise route or details of the destination (although God did), but he went in obedience. In doing so, he was responding to someone outside himself, to a higher authority, not merely to some inner desire to travel, still less to escape.

When the Israelite pilgrims went up to Jerusalem to worship in the temple, as they did three times a year, they did so because God had commanded their presence (Exodus 23:14–17; Deuteronomy 16:16). During the Feasts of Unleavened Bread, of Weeks and of Tabernacles they were required to appear before the Lord and visit the temple, the place in which he dwelt. It is these journeys that are captured in Psalm 84 and the Psalms of Ascents (Psalms 120–134), which the pilgrims sang as they approached Jerusalem and from which we can learn so much about pilgrimage.

Literal pilgrimages soon provided God's people with a new vocabulary for the whole of life. Jacob could look back on his life and describe it as 130 years of pilgrimage (Genesis 47:9). While others, especially the prophet Isaiah, could use the image time and again to envisage the return of God's people from exile in Babylon and their resettlement in a restored Jerusalem.

Pilgrims travel in formation

A party of tourists is usually a purely accidental arrangement of people who have never met each other before their holiday and, in many cases, have no desire to meet each other again once the holiday is over. They are thrown together on the journey and endure the efforts of the courier to manufacture camaraderie by means of enforced jollity. When they reach their destination they share the same hotel and go on the same expensive trips for the duration. Occasionally they really click with each other, but more often than not they don't, for, apart from being on this particular holiday together, they probably have very little in common. They are a purely transient group of people who happen to be travelling together on this occasion, but they could never be said to be a community, a brotherhood or even a meaningful group.

A band of pilgrims is altogether different; at least, the biblical pilgrims were. They had shared values and beliefs, and it was these that meant they travelled together as a meaningful group to the destination they had unitedly set their hearts on reaching. They belonged together because of their desire to reach Jerusalem and enter the presence of God. Psalm 84:1–4 expresses something of that yearning.

All sorts flowed from this collective consciousness. It meant they looked out for one another, stuck with one another in the tough parts of the journey, sang songs of encouragement to one another, relied on one another, provided for one another and inspired one another. The psalms of the pilgrims, seen most evidently as we have said in the Psalms of Assents, give evidence of this. Although some of them use 'I' and are personal, the dominant impression we are left with is of 'we' and 'our'. It is corporate not individual. They are about the tribes going up to Jerusalem (Psalm 122:1–4), the contempt they had collectively endured from others (Psalm 123:3–4) and the celebration of their release from captivity (Psalm 126:1–4). They are about 'Israel' (e.g. Psalms 128:5; 130:7–8), not about a collection of individual worshippers who happen to bump into one another on the road.

This vision of God's people travelling together in formation crosses over into the New Testament and is central to its vision for the church. Christianity is not about individual discipleship but about travelling on 'the Way' (which was one name for early Christianity [see Acts 9:2; 19:23; 22:4; 24:14, 22]) with one another. Think of all that we are called to do 'with one another'. We are not only to greet one another but accept, encourage, love, be devoted to, submit to, provide hospitality for, stimulate, and admonish one another.[23] It gives rise to the picture of the church as the army of the Holy Spirit, where the soldiers keep in step not only with him but with each other.[24]

---

23 The principal New Testament references are: Romans 12:10, 16; 13:8; 14:13; 15:7, 14; 16:16; 1 Corinthians 1:10; 16:20; 2 Corinthians 13:12; Galatians 5:13; Ephesians 4:2; Colossians 3:16; 1 Thessalonians 5:11; Hebrews 3:13; 10:24, 25; James 4:11; 1 Peter 1:22; 3:8; 4:9; 5:5, 14; 1 John 1:7; 3:11, 23; 4:7; 2 John 1:5.
24 Both Galatians 5:25–6:5 and Colossians 2:5 use collective, military terminology.

Many contemporary disciples of Jesus have been influenced too much by the mentality of the tourist, and just as they want to be 'consumers of church' they also want to demonstrate the semi-detached, not-quite-involved mentality of the tourist in their relationships with their fellow believers. They prefer a solo journey to their destination, with only an occasional bit of hitch-hiking thrown in at their convenience to the travelling in formation; in the committed, covenanted relationships that characterise the journey of pilgrims.

Pilgrims produce a transformation

In a way tourists have an effect on the places through which they travel. Having grown up in one of Britain's leading holiday resorts, I know. Of course, they contribute to the economy and to employment. But what's left when they've gone home? Usually nothing but a load of litter to clear up. Out come the road sweepers and refuse collectors to remove the tons of discarded fish-and-chip papers, sweet wrappers and unwanted newspapers that have been carelessly thrown to the ground.

In describing the journey to Jerusalem, Psalm 84:6 gives us a different picture of the transforming effect pilgrims had on their environment. It says, 'As they pass through the Valley of Baca, they make it a place of springs; the autumn rains also cover it with pools.' To make any sense of that we need to know that the Valley of Baca was known as the place where Balsa trees grew, and Balsa trees grow in very arid places. Here, then, is a picture of pilgrims transforming the places through which they travel for good. Because of them, desert places blossom, arid places become well watered and barren places become fruitful. So when tourists go home, all that is left is rubbish. When pilgrims go home, the world has been transformed into a better, more fertile and more wholesome place.

Psalm 84, of course, is not simply describing what once happened. It is telling us that this is what pilgrims do. It sets before us our contemporary mandate. The desert wastelands of our culture and the arid wilderness of postmodernity should be transformed by the presence of the pilgrims who are passing through. Previous generations of pilgrims achieved transformation. The children of the Reformation and their heirs in the evangelical movement of the eighteenth and nineteenth centuries accomplished amazing transformations of society – spiritually, morally, educationally, scientifically and in many other ways. Their impact, because they saw themselves as pilgrims, was enormous. The challenge before us is to have an equal impact in transforming our time, rather than being tourists who either leave our world just as we found it or, even worse, take from it and contribute to its decay without doing anything to change it for the better.

Pilgrims demonstrate a determination

The life of the tourist is easy, even if we do find plenty to complain about. The ease with which we travel in our jet planes and air-conditioned coaches was unimaginable to my grandparents' generation. We are conducted from our temperature-controlled hotels into our comfortable vehicles only to be disgorged into another desirable hotel at our next stop. We are sheltered at all times from the extremes of the natural environment and cared for in a humanly created one. Food, drink, ice-creams and entertainment are laid on in advance. The way opens up before us smoothly without our having to worry. The tour company has arranged it all. And, if Bauman is right, the slightest inconvenience or inclemency of weather means the tourist will just move on to somewhere more congenial.

Not so the pilgrim. The journey to Jerusalem was arduous. It involved many dangers for which there was no ready-made human protection. The burning midday sun could be unbearable. The chill, dark valleys where the sun never penetrated could be terrifying. Water could be scarce. Wild animals could be dangerous. Even without these, the journey would be arduous enough with no motorways to travel and only desert paths to follow and mountain ranges to climb. And then, when one got to Jerusalem, there was still the hill to ascend on which the city was built. Pilgrimage required stamina. It was not for the feeble, nor for those who would get easily discouraged. Psalm 84:5, 7 hints as much. A real desire to see God is required if you are not to give up halfway. It is something you should set your heart on. Strength is required to complete it. But those who have such a determination find themselves going from 'strength to strength'.

True, God provides for pilgrims and watches over them to keep them safe.[25] But that in no way detracts from the determination pilgrims themselves must show. Christian pilgrimage still requires determination.[26] There are plenty of disappointments and distractions to throw us off course. It does not fit easily with the transient, episodic nature of identity we have mentioned above. But it's no good being a

---

25 That is the subject of Psalm 121.
26 A classic expression of this is found in John Bunyan's, *Pilgrim's Progress* (many editions).

revolutionary in one's teens, a disciple of Jesus in one's 20s and a materialist in one's 30s. Jesus said, 'No-one who puts his hand to the plough and looks back is fit for service in the kingdom of God' (Luke 9:62). He also said on more than one occasion that those who stand firm to the end will be saved (Matthew 10:22; 24:13).

Being a Christian pilgrim does not mean we have been invited to join a packaged holiday to heaven. It means we're committed to making the journey with all the perseverance and determination we can muster: enduring all the hardships, rejecting all the distractions, avoiding what dangers we can and keeping going until we reach our destination.

Pilgrims aim for a destination

In one sense, tourists seem to have destinations. They dream of the golden shores of the Caribbean or the sun-drenched islands of the Mediterranean. But in another sense, as Bauman stresses, their destination is not so fixed. This year Italy, next year Majorca. And on holiday, time is empty and space is there to be filled. Today the beach, tomorrow the vineyard (perhaps), and (maybe) the next day the shops. Let's just keep moving to fill the time with one excitement after another. There is no real fixed, ultimate destination. Tourists wander. Tourists meander. But pilgrims have a set intention, a direction, a destination to reach. They're both on a journey. But the pilgrim alone passes through time and space with a purpose in mind and a future that determines the direction taken in the present.

In Psalm 84:7, the destination of the pilgrims is spoken of as appearing before God in Zion. Christian pilgrims share the same goal of wanting to appear before God.

John writes of our needing to 'remain in him . . . so that when he appears we may be confident and unashamed before him at his coming' (1 John 2:27–28). The sense of preparing ourselves to appear before God permeates the whole of the New Testament writings. A variety of images are pressed into use to amplify it. We need to run the race in such a way that we win the prize (1 Corinthians 9:24). We must stand before the judgement seat of Christ to give an account of our lives (2 Corinthians 5:10). We must keep ourselves as a pure virgin in readiness for marriage to Christ (2 Corinthians 11:2). We must recognise that Christ gave himself for the church, 'to make her holy . . . and to present her to himself as a radiant church, without stain or wrinkle or any other blemish, but holy and blameless' (Ephesians 5:25–27). We must press on to the city whose builder and maker is God (Hebrews 11:8–10, 16, 24–27).

Qualified for access to the presence of God through the cross of Christ, pilgrims are now to work towards their destination of appearing in his presence as a holy people, with all the determination they can muster. We are not called just to fill space and time but to use it so that we can become more and more like Christ in our character, be part of a church that is more and more pleasing to him and live our lives in a way that is more and more honouring to him.

Tourism may be bad news for morality. It's even worse news for spirituality. But pilgrimage isn't.

Zygmunt Bauman recognises that the metaphor of the pilgrim would characterise the way people used to live more appropriately than that of the tourist. But today the pilgrim has been supplanted by the tourist. Today, he writes, 'the world is not hospitable to pilgrims anymore'.[27] They don't fit. They're yesterday's men and women. The sense of serious purpose they displayed has been replaced by a sense of pleasure and fun. The sense of orderliness, sacrifice and determination that sets aside short-term gains for long-term rewards has been replaced by a desire to escape being boxed in, by a refusal to be fixed and by a quest for instant satisfactions and immediate rewards. The sense of preparing for an eternal future has been displaced by seeking fulfilment in a transient present.

But so what? Pilgrims have never been welcome in this world. They have always been strangers here, even while transforming the place for the better (see 1 Peter 1:1). The fact that being a tourist is more acceptable today than being a pilgrim should be neither here nor there for disciples of Jesus. Their lot is always to be the nonconformists. There are more important questions to face than those of our personal comfort or our cultural fit. We need to ask whether it is tourists or pilgrims who will build a better world. We need to ask whether it is tourists or pilgrims who will prepare best for eternity. We need to ask whether it is tourists or pilgrims who please God most. We need to ask whether we're called to be tourists or pilgrims. When we do, surely we see that being a pilgrim is better by far.

---

27 Bauman, *Life in Fragments*, p. 88.

6.

Settlers or Pioneers?

The last metaphor we will explore is a little different from the others. Rather than being one from our own time it reaches back to the days when the American frontier was being evangelised.

The early established colonies in New England were often founded by people who wished to escape religious persecution in the old world and practise their denominational faith in freedom. Congregationalism came to dominate, and by 1776 'the Congregationalists, Episcopalians, and Presbyterians seemed to be *the* colonial denominations'.[1] They probably never had the number of people worshipping with them that some of the myths that tell us America was founded as a godly nation would like us to believe. But even if they had, it wasn't long before entirely new problems faced them. New territory was soon explored and pioneers began to move west in search of

---

1 Roger Finke and Rodney Stark, *The Churching of America 1776–1990* (Rutgers University Press, 1992), p. 55.

gold or other ways of making their fortune. The mainline churches of New England were ill-equipped to evangelise or even pastor these pioneers. The established churches were led by well-qualified scholarly pastors, whose training had been expensive and whose upkeep in manses and church buildings was even more expensive. They cast their vote with the settlers, chose to stay in 'civilised' areas, performing their well-developed religious liturgies, and were indifferent to the needs of the pioneers. They began to decline in significance, at least as far as the total American religious scene was concerned.

Onto the stage, however, stepped the Methodists and Baptists – the Upstart Sects as they have been called.[2] They proved to be much less demanding about what was needed before they could function and much more adaptable than their venerable colleagues in the mainline churches. They needed no expensive theological college education, nor proper salaries, nor chapel buildings before they went out to win the West for Christ. They were common folk who 'spoke in the vernacular, and preached from the heart'.[3] These denominations, in so far as they existed, had low overheads and could respond to need in an immediate and versatile way. New forms of church arose, most of which were associated with the revival meeting and the camp meeting.

Traditionalists in the mainline denominations, of whom there were plenty, looked contemptuously at the efforts of these upstarts. But the fact is that while the established denominations declined, the Upstart Sects grew and made

---

2 See *ibid.*, where the story is told in detail.

3 *ibid.*, p. 77.

an enormous impact for the gospel of Christ. America became more, not less, religious than it ever had been in its history. Such progress would never have happened if it had depended on the inflexible, unbending established churches who sought to preserve a way of doing church that was precious to them. It happened because some were prepared to change. It happened because some threw off the cloak of the settlers and became pioneers.

The present challenge

The most obvious fact about the church in the United Kingdom today is that it is in decline. From the mid-1950s the decline has been fairly rapid and, although there have been occasional glimmers of hope, the trend has proved hard to counter. Scotland and Northern Ireland have staved off decline longer than England and Wales, but the symptoms of decline are now unmistakably there as well. The state of play was well summed up in the title of a recent article written by one expert in the field, called 'Christianity in Britain, R.I.P.'.[4] At the same time another scholar published a book with the title *The Death of Christian Britain*.[5] What the church stands for and what the church does seems to many to belong to a past age that they have no desire to recall.

People's rejection of the church is obviously connected with their rejection of the gospel and their preference for living without God. In one sense that has never been any

---

4 Steve Bruce, 'Christianity in Britain, R.I.P.', *Sociology of Religion: a quarterly review* 62.2 (2001) 191–203.
5 Callum Brown, *The Death of Christian Britain* (Routledge, 2001).

different and will always be the case. But in addition to these spiritual factors, there are also some social and cultural factors at work.

The changes we are undergoing are certainly wider than the church. Many traditional institutions that people were once proud to join are now in decline. Party political membership, trades union membership, membership of voluntary organisations such as the Scouts, some sporting activities and, periodically, even cinema attendances have all declined. The truth is that in comparison with some of these the church has fared well and declined less rapidly. Something bigger is going on, outside the church, which affects the way people express their belonging. It's different from how it used to be. And unless the church adapts, humanly speaking, the church as we know it will die.

Many within the church may well feel it has changed enough in recent years. Indeed, some blame the decline on the changes it has already made. If only it had been left as it was, when clergy were recognisably clergy, when we sang good old-fashioned hymns, preached good (and long) old-fashioned hell-fire sermons, prayed in 'thees' and 'thous' and read the Authorised Version, we wouldn't be in the mess we're in today, they say. But gone are most of the ladies' hats, the Sunday suits and the clergy robes. Gone is the majestic language of yesteryear. Gone is the solemn and sonorous organ. Gone is the commitment people showed to the weekly choir rehearsal or to running the youth club. In their place we dress casually, chat to God as if he were the boy next door, sing along to guitars, consume tit-bit, sound-bite sermons and throw ourselves into things only if they've a short shelf-life. If only things hadn't changed, some feel!

The evidence, however, proves such people wrong. There are enough churches around that have not changed to test their theory out. The fact is that with a very few notable exceptions, traditionalist churches that have stuck rigidly to a conservative style of worship and programme have experienced decline along with the rest, and in many cases more rapidly than those that have begun to adapt. Burying their stylistic heads in the sand has not saved them from the ice-chill winds of unbelief and social change that have affected us all. On the contrary, there is a good deal of evidence to show that churches of all denominations that have adapted have experienced growth, with the newly founded churches being just one of the examples proving the point. It's the experience of frontier America all over again. When it comes to mission, settlers lose out and pioneers gain.

Is it OK to change the church?

In addition to the normal reasons why we resist change and feel more secure with what is familiar, many feel the church should not be changed because the way we do it is the way it should be done; it's biblical. Their normal resistance to change is therefore compounded by spiritual overtones. Such resistance is misplaced. The Bible would actually encourage us in the opposite direction.

What the Bible undermines: faith in unchangeable church structures

Jeremiah once preached a famous sermon that has become known as 'the temple sermon'. In it he says, 'Do not trust in deceptive words and say, "This is the temple of the

Lord, the temple of the Lord."' (Jeremiah 7:4). His point was that the Jews thought themselves safe from harm and immune to the political and social changes going on around them because they were devoted to worshipping in the temple and observing its religious rituals. Their moral lives, however, were far from pleasing to God. And because of that they were to experience God's judgement through the coming exile. Trusting in the physical and ritual structures of the temple could never preserve them from that. It could not make them immune from God's discipline. Their faith should have been in the living God and his word rather than in lifeless stones and immutable ceremonies. Our faith is still misplaced if it is in church structures.

Stephen made that point very clearly in the moving but provocative speech he made to the Jewish Council, which led to his execution. He reminded them, 'the Most High does not live in houses made by human hands'.[6] The centre of their faith was not to be a building in Jerusalem and what went on in it. It was to be a living person, the Righteous One. Indeed, not many years later the temple was destroyed and could no longer be looked to as the centre of the Jewish faith.

What the Bible underlines: commitment to flexible structures

To put the positive case, the Bible demonstrates that the people of God have always been flexible in constructing structures and patterns of worship to suit their changing circumstances. At least four major and different models

---

6 Acts 7:48, echoing words God spoke to David in 1 Chronicles 17:4 and Solomon's prayer of dedication of the temple in 2 Chronicles 6:18.

are distinguishable within the Bible, with the last one embracing a range of sub-models within it.[7]

A tabernacle community in the wilderness   First, the people of God formed a *tabernacle community*. After Egypt they lived in the wilderness and were on a journey to the Promised Land. They lived in tents that could be dismantled and erected with relative ease. It was appropriate, then, that their worship facility was a large tent, erected according to God's design and placed in the middle of the camp. His dwelling was the one around which all their life revolved. The worship they practised in the tent was largely sacrificial, although there were elements of understanding the law, intercession and discerning the will of God involved as well. In explaining why he refused David permission to build a temple, God said through Nathan the prophet,

> I have not dwelt in a house from the day I brought Israel up out of Egypt to this day. I have moved from one tent site to another, from one dwelling-place to another. Wherever I have moved with all the Israelites, did I ever say to any of their leaders whom I commanded to shepherd my people, 'Why have you not built me a house of cedar?' (1 Chronicles 17:5–6)

The mobile structure was appropriate for a pilgrim people and their living, active God.

A temple community in the land   When they entered the

---

7   For a scholarly exposition of this theme as it relates to the Old Testament see Walter Brueggemann, 'Rethinking Church Models through Scripture', *Theology Today* XLVIII.2 (1991) 128–38.

land, however, such a structure was no longer necessary and was ill-suited to their urban environment. So, under the monarchy, the people of God became a *temple community*. The city of Jerusalem became God's dwelling place and at its heart Solomon built a magnificent and permanent sanctuary for his glory. Worship remained essentially sacrificial, with a round of daily and annual offerings being presented to God. It wasn't as easy for people to participate as frequently as they once did, since they were now spread throughout the land and some distance from the shrine. Consequently thrice-yearly pilgrimages came to be significant with the priests offering year-round sacrifices on their behalf. Centralised worship had its own dangers, just as dispersed worship had. It concentrated power in the hands of a religious elite, the priesthood, who came to abuse their position, not least because they were a bit too close to the monarch, whom they served as court chaplains. Hence prophets arose to try to prevent the worship of Israel from becoming corrupted – a spiritual liability instead of an asset. The evidence of Jeremiah's temple sermon, as well as the writings of many of the other prophets, was that they failed to stem the dangers inherent in temple worship. Nonetheless, at its best the temple provides us with another model by which the people of God organise their religious life.

A textual community in the exile   Their failure to keep covenant faith with God led to the long nightmare of the exile. Transported, as it were, to the other side of their known world, with their temple lying in ruins and their city razed to the ground, the people of God faced a new challenge. How can you worship God in Babylon when there is no temple in which to do so and no possibility of offering animals in sacrifice? The answer was to be found in another model of religious community: they became a *textual community*. They may not have been able to offer sacrifices, but they could study the law and seek to interpret it and apply it to their new situation. Prayer groups emerged, which met around the Scriptures. New markers, like the observance of the sabbath, became even more important. If there was no sacred space they could visit to worship, they could at least set aside some sacred time – a new type of space – to worship and meditate on sacred scrolls. Even when they were eventually able to return to Jerusalem and build the temple once again they never left behind the idea of being a textual community. The exile meant that from then on they were to be a more dispersed people, and one version of the textual community came to be seen in the synagogues that were found wherever there was a Jewish population to speak of. We see all this reflected in Jesus' day, both through his visits to the synagogues and having to deal with the scribes or the teachers of the law. They now became the religious experts in Israel, along with the priests.

A transformed, transnational community in Christ The people of God of the new covenant emerged from these roots, but the gospel led them to organise their common life differently from what had gone on before. In Jesus they became a *transformed and transnational community*. No longer were ten men needed to form a worshipping community but only two or three (Matthew 18:20). Although for a little while, as the early chapters of Acts show us, the Jewish believers in Jesus still worshipped at the temple and the synagogue, Acts 2:42–47; 4:23–37 and 6:1–6 show that they struck out in new directions as well. They made use of homes, engaged in prayer, listened to the apostles teach about the new faith, shared in bread and wine together, sang psalms and hymns, rejoiced in mutual, practical support and felt entirely free to reorganise the leadership structures of their fellowship as they felt appropriate. The honest truth is that we know very little about how they organised their common or worship life together. The New Testament is much more concerned to tell us about the characters that filled the structures than give us details of the structures themselves. We know little of their leadership structures, which seem to have been fairly adaptable according to their circumstances.

We can legitimately draw the inference that there was a difference in feel between those churches that were predominantly Jewish in background and those that were predominantly Gentile. The latter, like Corinth, threw up new questions for Paul because of the absence of any moral background in the Jewish law, and because of their exercise of charismatic gifts and emphasis on the participation of their members. Each community of believers in Jesus, however, broke down the accepted barriers that divided the world, whether ethnic, social or gender divisions, and modelled what a community of reconciliation would be like.

The people of God, then, have always been flexible in the way they organised their common life. In Walter Brueggemann's words:

There is no single or normative model of church life . . . models of the church must not be dictated by cultural reality, but they must be voiced and practised in ways that take careful account of the particular time and circumstance into which God's people are called. Every model of church must be critically contextual.[8]

So the point is . . .

The churches we have inherited today would probably be unrecognisable to our early Christian forebears. Special buildings, authorised clergy, wooden pews, accepted liturgies (whether formally or informally recognised) and our 'correct orders' would seem to them to be very strange.[9] The truth is that our way of being church has far more to do with nineteenth-century British culture than with essential and non-negotiable biblical principles. The way the nineteenth-century British civil service organised the country (or, in the case of the Free Churches, provincial town politics, with which nonconformity was often closely enmeshed) had a potent formative influence on our churches.

Take an example: in congregationally governed churches, that is churches like the Baptists and many Free evangelical churches, the common life of the church is governed by the church meeting. Biblical precedents are to be found in places like Acts 6 and 15 and 1 Corinthians 5. But those passages give us sparse details of how they actually did things. In recent years we have frequently been told that to do things 'decently and in order', as they would have done

---

8 Walter Brueggemann, *Cadences of Home* (Westminster John Knox Press, 1997), p. 100f.

9 It is true that Paul argues that worship 'should be done in a fitting and orderly way' (1 Corinthians 14:40), but the point he is making is against rudeness, self-centredness and chaos in worship, not that one bureaucratic way of organising church is correct.

then, there are rules of procedures to be followed. Apologies of absence have to be recorded, minutes of the previous meeting read, matters arising discussed, propositions proposed and seconded, and votes taken and recorded. Truth to tell, none of that has a precedence in Scripture. Most of it finds precedence in the high days of nonconformist/liberal politics of the late nineteenth century. And there seem to be some real curiosities involved. Why should those who are not present have their names recorded in the minutes under 'apologies for absence' while those who are present, and therefore responsible for the decisions taken, get away without their names being recorded, since the usual practice is simply to record the number (not the names) of those present? Surely it's *their* names that should be in the minutes – they're the guilty ones!

Take another very different, albeit trivial, example, which has to do with more general cultural trends. Is it possible to worship God without having flowers in the church? I have known several incidents that would lead me to suspect not. The person on the flower rota has forgotten their duty and, horror of horrors, people turn up to church to find the sanctuary bare. Panic sets in. Several women scurry around to secure some form of foliage or decoration, even plastic flowers (ugh!) to adorn 'the house of God'. They obviously fear he may not turn up if the flowers are not present. The truth is that beautifying our places of worship like this would have been anathema to some of our forebears. It was only with the onset of the romantic movement, which gave a much more positive evaluation of creation and nature than previously, that flowers were allowed in church. Before long they became indispensable aids to worship. Now one suspects that a stranger who knew nothing of our practices might conclude that while preparing to worship by bringing holy lives and prayerful, expectant attitudes was optional, flowers were essential!

So the way we do church now is highly influenced by the culture of previous generations. We've become settlers and what the gospel and world needs is pioneers. The Lausanne Congress on World Evangelisation, held in 1974, recognised this. Its Covenant has proved to be a document of major significance in world missions and one of the best biblically grounded statements about mission in the history of the church. It affirms the importance of the church in evangelism and then, in Clause 10, discusses the relationship between culture and mission. It is a balanced statement, which argues that no culture should be uncritically accepted. Some might actually be demonic, while others may be rich in beauty and goodness and more naturally suitable vehicles for the gospel. The clause begins like this:

> The development of strategies for world evangelisation calls for imaginative pioneering methods. Under God, the result will be the rise of churches *deeply rooted in Christ and closely related to their culture.*[10]

Twenty-seven years later that still seems to me the challenge facing the British church. Both aspects are vital. A church that is culturally well adapted but has lost its roots in Christ is of no value to anyone. It might be a very exciting place to be, but it is worse than worthless as far as any

---

10 J. D. Douglas (ed.), *Let the Earth Hear His Voice* (World Wide Publications, 1975), p. 6f, italics mine.

eternal judgements are concerned. But a church that has its roots in Christ must also be culturally adapted. In fact, it is questionable whether you can have your roots deep into Christ unless you are well related to the culture in which you are placed, since Christ demonstrated in his own incarnation that God works not abstractly but in and through a particular time and cultural setting. If we are to follow in Christ's footsteps we too will be 'incarnate' in our culture. Given this, we need pioneers, not settlers, to lead the church today.

So, what's changed?

In recent years several perceptive Christian thinkers have come to our aid in understanding the changes we are currently going through in our culture. Among them are John Drane, Eddie Gibbs and Michael Moynagh.[11] They are not only good thinkers but have an ability to write at a popular and accessible level for non-academics. My own way of spelling out the changes, none of which are to be accepted uncritically, goes something like this:

From programme to people   The church has been a highly organised and busy place to be, with an activity for every conceivable age group and gender, all of whom organise their own programme, elect their own officers and make their own report to the wider church or even to an outside national body. Often there has been little room for people

---

11 John Drane, *Faith in a Changing Culture* (HarperCollins, 1997), Eddie Gibbs and Ian Coffey, *Church Next* (IVP, 2001) and Michael Moynagh, *Changing World, Changing Church* (Monarch, 2001).

in this. We've been too busy for them. They have had to fit with our programme.

From institution to community   People used to be joiners of societies. They wanted to belong and participate in the management of voluntary organisations. People are too busy for that now. They want to pay others to run things, and find the formal business and institutional side of life boring. They have a consumer mentality and look to service providers to give them what they want. (It has happened in sports as well as in church. Hence the decline of old community leagues and the rise of health and fitness clubs.) Yet people do want to belong, to relate and to be accepted for what they are as individuals, rather than being cloned as members. They are still searching for community.

From dogmatism to spirituality   The church of the past was composed of those who shared (at least said they shared) a common statement of faith and a common pattern of behaviour. The behaviour usually expressed itself not only in the virtues of self-discipline, clean living and integrity, but in a particular pattern of family life as well. The nuclear family became the ideal. Today people seem impatient with restricted codes of belief and behaviour. Yet they are searching for, and in many cases finding, spiritual experiences that feed the inner being. McDonald's-type worship, as we have mentioned, fails to engage with such people. Since few have conventional church backgrounds they have often not been schooled in conventional Christian morality and lifestyle and, at least on first encounter with the church, find it judgemental rather than accepting. Different family arrangements are becoming the norm and people want them accepted by the church.

From understanding to feeling Putting the last point in different words we might say that people today are not so concerned about understanding the logical, abstract propositions and ideas of the faith. They don't want to know in theory about God. They want to feel him in their worship and experience him in their lives. So courses on signs and wonders are likely to be more popular than courses on the theology of Paul. Narrative (story-telling) preaching is likely to be more popular than propositional preaching. Pictures received from God, there and then, may be taken as seriously, if not more so, than anything the Bible says.

From evangelism to worship The missions in which the church used to engage have largely fallen out of fashion. In them the truth would be proclaimed to unbelievers, usually by an 'expert', with the purpose of persuading them to believe. Nowadays people don't like to be preached at, especially by so-called experts. They want to discover things for themselves, through their own experience. Belonging comes before believing. A sense of belonging grows as people experience the church at worship. They would rather see the goods on offer than only be told about them before finally signing up.

From compartmentalisation to wholeness Spiritual life used to be concerned almost exclusively with spiritual things. It was what one did at church. Indeed, the church's programme was so all-encompassing that one rarely had time to do anything else, even if one wanted to. So it was good on prayer, witnessing, holiness of life, even family issues. But it rarely touched business ethics, political issues, leisure pursuits (except to condemn them) or environmental questions. Now people refuse to compartmentalise the faith. Spirituality is about planet earth and our own bodies as much as 'holy things'.

From verbal to visual The old world was a book-centred world; the new one is visual and IT centred. On entering many churches the first thing one is given is a collection of hymn books, prayer books and notice sheets. The liturgy and sermon are full of words. Today people have grown accustomed to learning by watching and seeing as much as, if not more than, hearing. Fast-moving images communicate where slow-moving words once painstakingly did their job.

From mass-produced to tailor-made Paradoxically, in the world of McDonald's, Ford is out, Starbucks is in. Ford cars were mass-produced. 'You can have any colour as long as it's black.' Now choice is in. You can't get a straightforward coffee these days. You have to negotiate a complex menu so that you get one tailor-made to your taste. The church used to mass-produce. One style of worship and learning was made to fit all. But now people want to choose their style of worship, their style of learning and when they will do it. Cell groups within church can help that.

From national to local Identifying with remote national bodies is unpopular. What's real is local. No longer are people concerned about what denominational label the church has; what matters is whether they feel at home in it, whatever the label. While many churches feel ill at ease in giving to some national mission fund or sending their members overseas through some national mission agency, many will give just as much as they ever did directly to causes they know and send their members directly overseas to churches and situations with whom they have links. Flexible networking has replaced traditional denominational loyalties.

From static to mobile   Traditional church assumed a largely static community. People lived in the parish and, since they had the time, could be relied on to run the youth group or turn up at the choir practice every week. Now people travel. They travel to work; they travel to visit; they travel to move house. They're not at home as much as they used to be. They're not in the community as often as they used to be because they're off visiting friends or relatives (probably friends!). They're not going to be a member of your church for as long as they once would have been. So more things have to be done for people. More things have to be done on a short-term, intensive basis. And the church has to be much quicker at getting to know people and using them than it once was.

I have only been able to paint the above patterns with broad brush strokes. Each of these contrasts is complex and, if I had the time and space, I would want to qualify every one. Not everyone is making the transitions at the same pace. Some parts of the country are much slower to change. But in the end we're all affected by the major engines of our society, like the media, consumer brands and IT, which will move us all on. Let me emphasise again that not all of these trends are to be welcomed uncritically. But, equally, nor are they to be uncritically opposed, just because they involve change. Each of them is to be considered carefully and each of them invites us to think afresh what it means to be church, faithfully serving God, today.

So what might the church of the future look like?[12]

Forecasting the future is a dangerous job and most people get it wrong. I am encouraged that governments, who pour huge resources into planning for what is to come, frequently fail to get it right. Already, however, new patterns of church are beginning to emerge and we're beginning to envisage some possible scenarios. In drawing attention to some of the new forms of church I am not saying these are the patterns we must slavishly follow. My purpose is to stir the imagination and encourage creative thinking. My first introduction to Willow Creek Community Church, the remarkable seeker-driven church for the young upwardly mobile in Chicago, was liberating in this respect for me. One of the staff stressed that no one there wanted clones of Willow Creek to be created around the world, although they did want the questions they had asked and principles on which they worked to be taken seriously. Rather, he said, Willow Creek wanted to be a 'model of permission'; that is, a model which said that church could be done differently for the glory of God. So what are the models of permission here?

---

12 The best and fullest survey is found in Moynagh, *Changing World, Changing Church*.

Shopping mall church   The church might come to resemble a shopping mall more. Under the one roof, different niche groups might meet to worship and learn to be disciples. Since one size no longer fits all, different generations or ethnic groups might each worship while acknowledging that they belong together. Different styles of music and different styles of learning can be accommodated in this way. Such a church raises questions about how real the unity we are supposed to have found in Christ is.

Midweek church   People's real relationships are formed in the workplace, not in their neighbourhoods. Church members often do not know their neighbours (at least once the kids have left the local junior school) and have little in common with them. In this respect they are not very different from their non-Christian neighbours. They don't know anyone either. But they do know the people in the workplace with whom they spend hours every day. Some are beginning to make that their natural place to worship and learn the faith together. Why not a church for taxi-drivers, or a church for those who work in a particular firm? It makes for a church that is much more related to the everyday issues than the detached churches of suburbia. And it frees people for family and other commitments at weekends. But, of course, it only involves those who work there, not their partners and children.

Seeker church   Willow Creek has been the pioneer model here in our generation, though it has been pointed out, rightly in my view, that all they have done is what the evangelistic missions of D. L. Moody and Billy Graham did in their day. They are providing a context in which people might learn about the gospel in a package that is culturally comfortable to them. Hence, at Willow Creek there is an emphasis on drama and music, and a playing down of the more traditionally religious aspects of worship, like the singing of hymns (although preaching has remained a major element of their services). Everything they do aims at excellence, for excellence marks the world in which their target audience – the people who live around them in South Barrington – lives. Amateurism is out. Other seeker-sensitive churches would look very different if they were built around trying to win a different target audience for Christ. Care needs to be taken to cater for the growth of those who are believers so as to avoid winning converts who never grow up in Christ. At Willow Creek this takes place through 'New Community' worship services, which are held midweek and through a vigorous small group programme.

Youth church Already Britain boasts a number of youth churches, some of which have been around so long they are facing the problem of no longer being attended by young people! They all style themselves differently according to the particular youth sub-culture they attract. Some have a nightclub feel about them while others are much more traditional. Generally they relate to a slightly broader movement of alternative worship too, where the use of sound and light, imagination and arts, movement and IT are all used much more than in traditional churches.

Cell church Not to be mistaken for a church that runs home groups, cell church is a church that consciously arranges its life primarily around cells and disburses its leadership and life through them, coming together only weekly to worship in a celebration event. To belong to such a church is to belong to the cell first, and to be committed to the corporate discipleship of the cell. It's not a question of joining the church and then opting into a cell if you so decide. Alternatively, a cell church might consist of a single cell and meet in a pub, a home or some other local facility, but not a church. The danger might be that a single-cell church could become introverted and more easily go off the rails with wacky ideas because it lacks the steer that contact with the wider church provides. On the positive side, however, it provides the sense of community for which many are searching.

Church in the shopping mall   The church used to be at the heart of the community. That's why it is usually situated next door to the pub. The heart of the community is now more frequently to be found in the superstore or shopping mall. Some have begun to experiment with a church there. What an opportunity to reach people! Mums are only too delighted to park their kids for an hour. Together with running midweek latch-key or after-school clubs for children whose parents are still at work, this is a contemporary version of the old Sunday school.

So there are all sorts of ways in which church can be done differently. Those of us who are settlers should be challenged out of our comfort zones by the pioneers who are showing us the way, and support them as they seek to forge into new territory and construct new models appropriate for our day.

At this point, major reservations are usually voiced.

Aren't these new churches divisive? Don't they target one group to the exclusion of others? Don't they betray a failure to understand that our gospel is one of reconciliation while they perpetuate the ethnic, social, generational or cultural divisions of our society? Aren't they destroying the church? Hasn't it gone downhill since these new churches started? Don't they pander to a cheap consumerist type of Christianity?

Four brief responses might be given. First, as mentioned earlier, there is no evidence that churches refusing to change have been able to maintain their hold on existing members, let alone attract new ones. Decline set in well before new types of churches came into being.

Second, it is not only the newer types of church that appeal to different groups of people. They may be more honest about their desire to target particular groups but, in practice, most traditional churches unconsciously target particular groups and, by their way of doing things, alienate others. An unspoken process of self-selection has been at work. The church has frequently been implicitly exclusive. So the charge, which must be taken seriously, does not only apply to newer churches.

Third, there is the danger that all Christian groups will pander to a consumerist-type Christianity, not just the newer churches. All must question whether they are practising and preaching a Christianity that baptises the worldly quests of their members or whether they are living as and learning to be counter-cultural disciples of Jesus.

Fourth, the variety of churches already in existence, of different denominations and churchmanships, means that the church of God is already fragmented. That does not justify further fragmentation, but it does mean that all church members, whether from the older or the newer churches, must question what they mean when they talk of the unity of the church. Richard Baxter struggled with the question of church division way back in 1670. He worked as hard as anyone to maintain the unity of the church but asked that people would be realistic in their expectations of it. He took the view that, 'The church here is a hospital of diseased souls; of whom none are perfectly healed in this life.' He recognised that people would be at different levels of spiritual maturity and have different needs according to their age. He warned against the sins of pride, back-biting and judgementalism, and the danger of being manipulated by those who were more passionate about some things than others. And then he drew attention to the crucial issue. Where separation is considered the right way forward in practice, we must continue to recognise each other as part of the body of Christ and never disfellowship one another. In his words, '. . . if for any reason it is impossible to go on meeting together, it is still necessary to keep unity in faith and love. Spiritual condescension, let alone worse, is not permitted.'[13]

If it had not been for the spiritual pioneers who turned their back on the comfortable churchmanship of the settlers, the frontier regions of America would never have been won for Christ. The religious settlers looked on the pioneers with just the sort of condescension Baxter rules out. They considered their religion deficient in depth and decorum. But history records that they were effective in their mission, and under them America became a more

---

13 Richard Baxter, *The Cure of Church Divisions* (Nevile Symmonds, 1670), Clause 59.

godly nation. We face a new frontier – the frontier of post-Christian Britain. And we need new pioneers to conquer it for Christ.

Study Guide

1. 'Just Do It!' or 'Jesus Did It!'?

- Consider why designer labels such as Nike are so desirable. What does this suggest about human nature?
- Discuss the ways in which the Nike slogan, 'Just do it!', is appropriate advice for Christians (2 Chronicles 20:20 and Mark 11:22 might help you).
- What are the positive and negative effects that sport can have in the lives of Christians, locally and nationally? You might like to include in your thinking the work of Christians in Sport, who seek to reach and support those in sport.
- Why is Nike's emphasis on human potential, celebrity status and success a spiritually damaging influence?
- What issues might Jesus have raised with the chief executive of Nike if he had met him rather than Nicodemus? (John 3)

2. Magic Kingdom or Jesus' Kingdom?

- What are the dangers of the escapist nature of the contemporary entertainment world seen particularly in theme parks and computer games?
- How might your church or fellowship learn from Disney in terms of image and organisation? What could your church helpfully do better in terms of practical arrangement, decoration and physical atmosphere?
- Why do people choose the magic kingdom over the kingdom of Jesus?
- In what ways have Christians sold out to the magic kingdom, with the emphasis only on what is entertaining, fun and people-centred?
- Do Christians live in a fantasy world at church, where real issues such as abuse, addiction, immorality and broken relationships are kept hidden behind the scenery?

3. Fast-Food Junkies or Gourmet Connoisseurs?

- Is the eating of fast food 'morally inferior' to other ways of eating? Is style of eating a spiritual issue, since it is linked with issues of family, community and having time for each other?
- Would you agree with the contention that Christians are increasingly settling for fast-food spirituality, which is easy to digest, fun and offers short-term satisfaction but has only limited long-term value?
- In our evangelistic strategies and planning are there dangers in being too focused on the process rather than

the people God loves?

- Fast-food outlets emphasise efficiency. Is an efficient church a more spiritual church? In your discussion you might like to include the Parable of the Talents (Matthew 25:14–30) and the Parable of the Workers in the Vineyard (Matthew 20:1–16).

4. Consumers or Disciples?

- Suggest ways in which you could resist consumerism by buying only what you need and not what is the latest fashion.
- How far is choice both a positive and negative experience? Is choice in church life, being able to choose which church we go to, a good thing?
- Discuss what types of consumer behaviour master people. Consider how as a Christian you can avoid being mastered by unhelpful consumer attitudes. Reflect on 1 Corinthians 6:12 in your discussion.
- What is the difference between being a disciple and being a consumer? What aspects of discipleship clash most obviously with the consumer mentality? Use Matthew 16:24–26 as you think about the issue.

5. Tourists or Pilgrims?

- Is the environmental damage done to our world by business, industry, commerce and Western lifestyles evidence of our attitudes as tourists?
- If pilgrims are about transforming the land as they pass through, consider how your fellowship, small group or individual action could have a transforming

effect on the community in which you live.

- Why does the tourist mentality to life and spirituality appear to be an attractive option?
- How might you commit yourself more effectively to being a pilgrim in your faith and lifestyle?
- Where does the tourist mentality lead in the long term?

6. Settlers or Pioneers?

- Where Terah, Abraham's father, settled, he died (Genesis 11:31–32). What might the application of this example be to you today? How settled are you in your faith and attitudes?
- Imagine you are establishing a new congregation of about 50 believers. What would be your priorities for the life of this Christian community? In what ways could you be pioneering in worship, evangelism, discipleship and fellowship?
- Consider your current fellowship or church: is it pioneering or settled?
- Those who pioneered in America had an advantage in that they could not be settled but had to establish God's community. We are mostly part of settled and established fellowships. How can we avoid being too settled in our communities?
- Suggest three ways in which your church could pioneer faith relevantly in your local community. Use some of the current cultural issues of emphasising people, community, spirituality, feeling, worship, wholeness, visual, tailor-made, local and mobile.

Responding to the Challenge of Evolution

by Kevin Logan

A journalist and Anglican minister searches for the truth behind the jargon and polemics surrounding the theory of evolution as taught in our schools and preached on our television screens.

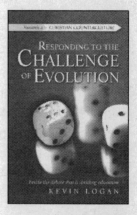

In doing so he

- listens to the experts on both sides of the debate

- picks up on the Gateshead controversy over teaching creationism in schools

- looks at arguments surrounding the 'young earth' and 'old earth' theories

This book will help you to clarify your thinking on this vital topic.